55 QUESTIONS TO ASK BEFORE YOU SELL YOUR BUSINESS

VALUE-DRIVING PRINCIPLES TO MAKE YOUR BUSINESS BETTER TODAY AND WHEN YOU SELL IT

HoganTaylor LLP
CPAs + ADVISORS

55 QUESTIONS TO ASK BEFORE YOU SELL YOUR BUSINESS

VALUE-DRIVING PRINCIPLES TO MAKE YOUR BUSINESS BETTER TODAY AND WHEN YOU SELL IT

ROBERT WAGNER

Published by HoganTaylor LLP
www.hogantaylor.com

HoganTaylor LLP
2222 S. Utica Pl., Ste. 200
Tulsa, OK 74114
www.hogantaylor.com

Library of Congress Control Number: 2021900121

ISBN: 978-1-7363936-0-4 (hardcover)
ISBN: 978-1-7363936-1-1 (paperback)
ISBN: 978-1-7363936-2-8 (e-book)

Book design by Justin Johnson

This book is dedicated to business owners and leaders who build great companies, solve complex problems, deliver world-class service, nurture and develop their employees to their maximum capabilities, and invest themselves and their capital into building a better world.

Table of Contents

Introduction

One day, your business will be owned by someone else. Your baby, your dream, the thing you have nurtured from infancy through great expansions, through near-death experiences, to what it is today, will be owned and led by someone else.

Only four things can happen to a business: it will be sold; it will be given to your kids while you are living; it will fail; or it will become part of your estate when you die, and then it will be sold, be given to your kids, or fail. Those are your choices.

This book is about taking control of this certainty and choosing the path that will provide the maximum value to you, the owner.

And let's be clear: you deserve the maximum value for the business you have built. Your business is a powerful force in the markets and communities you serve.

As a business owner, you are the most important ingredient in a thriving, prosperous, and free economy. Most of us are waiting for something to happen. We are waiting for someone like you to come along, start a business, and hire us to use our talents and skills. Without your willingness to invest your capital, take risks, do what few others are willing to do, and never give up on your goals—no matter the setbacks— our economy would decay and eventually die.

You pay all the bills in our economy. Period.

As a partner in a certified public accounting (CPA) firm, I frequently remind our staff that every bill, every piece of technology, every paycheck, and every bonus is paid by people like you, our client business owners.

You pay the taxes that fund our national security, our social service programs, and our national research and development efforts. Your charitable generosity, either through your direct gifts or your purchases of goods and services that enrich vendors and other business owners, is the catalyst that endows every building on college campuses, builds every place of worship of every faith, and funds a multitude of important causes to lift people out of despair and give them hope for the future.

For all these reasons, you deserve the maximum value for what you have created.

As the owner, you will likely enjoy many wonderful nonfinancial rewards when you sell your business. More free time, less stress, and the opportunity to dive deeply into important social causes will all be available to you once you are unencumbered from the responsibilities of leading. But you may also find great opportunity to reap significant, life-changing, even multigenerational wealth by selling the company you have created.

This book is about preparing for that process.

Why Read This Book?

Hopefully, you are reading this book long before you are ready to sell your business. If so, I can promise you a number of benefits:

- You will be ready if an unsolicited offer arrives in your inbox sooner than you expect;

- You will address now the issues you know need to be dealt with and are necessary to scale your business in the future;

- You will be encouraged to do the right thing in your business—a choice that is never wrong or premature;

- You and your business will enjoy a lower cost of capital because banks and other capital providers generally love the same things buyers do; and

- You will find maintaining your business less stressful as you build processes and habits that make it easier to run, easier to analyze, and more profitable in the long run.

There are many ingredients to value in the eyes of potential buyers. While some of those ingredients are based on the buyer's own strategy and goals, most are in your control.

While I hope you will spend at least one to three years preparing to sell your business, if instead you are seriously considering selling your business soon, this book will enable you to:

- Address in advance the issues that foster potential buyers' confidence that a transaction can be completed quickly;

- Analyze your business from a buyer's perspective, with less emotion and personal attachment;

- Assign value to the things that matter to most buyers; and

- Make your business more attractive than most of the other "deals" professional buyers are considering.

This book is for business owners and key advisors such as CPAs, legal counsel, and bankers who want to drive value into the owner's business, create an attractive company for acquisition, and provide assurance that a deal can be completed expeditiously. This book is also for chief financial officers (CFOs), controllers, and other executives of small and mid-sized businesses who want to know how to increase their businesses' value today and in the future.

The 55 Questions

The 55 Questions were born from my experience as a CFO of a publicly owned technology company that used acquisitions as a primary growth strategy, as well as my subsequent experience working as an outsourced CFO or transaction advisor.

In 1999 our company, XETA Technologies, Inc., was generating approximately $35 million in revenues selling and servicing a proprietary telecommunications device known as a call accounting system. We were also a dealer and service provider for Hitachi USA, selling their private branch exchange (PBX) systems. The company had also built a 24/7 service center taking care of the telecommunications needs of our 3,000 hotel customers in more than 40 states. We were the market leader in hotel telecommunications, and Marriott Hotels was our flagship customer.

We had a strong balance sheet and good cash flows and were enjoying our strongest growth ever as customers upgraded their systems to prepare for Y2K. In addition, the telecommunications industry was projected to undergo massive disruption because of the integration of voice and data networks into a single platform.

With these factors in place, we embarked on a two-pronged acquisition strategy to 1) expand our customer base outside of the hospitality industry and 2) enter the data networking business to be ready with professional services and productivity-generating applications, delivering on the promises of voice and data integration.

Within six months, we were starting due diligence on the potential acquisition of the largest dealer of Avaya PBX systems in the United States. This acquisition would double our revenues, add an entirely new product and service line to our portfolio, and expand our customer base beyond hospitality into many premium Fortune 1000 companies.

We were able to successfully close this transaction, and over time it delivered on its strategic goals. For us, the strategic potential of this transaction was so powerful that we looked past many of the issues we discovered in our due diligence process. We knew in fact that many potential buyers had looked at the target company and had elected not to pursue a purchase for a variety of reasons.

Although we moved forward on this transaction despite some big red flags, the target was a good example of a company that could have made itself more valuable and more saleable to a wider audience of potential buyers had it been willing to address a variety of internal issues.

As we moved forward with our acquisition strategy over the next ten years, we looked at dozens of companies, most of which were direct or indirect competitors. We passed on most but ultimately acquired about a dozen other companies.

In all those transactions, the findings of our due diligence process eroded the seller's value from the original offer. In several instances, this erosion had a meaningful impact on the overall transaction value. In those cases, the seller had to accept a lower price and/or provide additional safeguards, such as escrows, holdbacks, warranties, and earn-outs, to incentivize us to move forward with the transaction. As you will find out when you sell your business, once you have accepted a letter of intent, the negotiating leverage shifts to the buyer. From that moment forward, most changes in your business's value will be downward. Furthermore, the pressure on you to consummate the sale will be enormous as your mind shifts into your future "post-sale" life.

In 2011, XETA received an unsolicited offer from a competitor to purchase 100 percent of the stock of our company. The offer provided significant value to our shareholders over the current stock price, and the buyer had the financial backing to complete the transaction. Understanding those facts, our board of directors embarked on an auction process in which we hired an investment banker to cast a wide net to potential buyers. After a winnowing process, six companies participated in the auction by conducting extensive due diligence on our company, including site visits and hours-long meetings and teleconferences. In the end, two final bidders made firm offers.

The auction process took approximately eight months. It was both a grueling and professionally rewarding experience as potential suitors undertook a highly unemotional and detailed review of our company, giving us the opportunity to sell the potential buyers on its many strengths but also forcing us to deal with the realities of its weaknesses. We were able to close the transaction and deliver good value and an exit for our shareholders, some of whom were original sponsors of the company.

The process of selling our company brought to the forefront the importance of consistently working to improve your business.

The primary driver of business value will always be cash flows, but not all cash flows are created equal. Although historical cash flows are often a good predictor of future cash flows, buyers can only receive a return on their investment from future cash flows. Therefore, buyers must have supreme confidence that future cash flows are resilient, diversified, somewhat predictable, and scalable. Beyond these issues buyers want to understand a wide host of issues before they can justify writing the check that rewards you for a lifetime of effort of building your business.

The 55 Questions are organized into five groups:

- General Financial Questions

- Revenue and Profitability Questions

- Financial Condition and Capital Structure Questions

- Strategic, Organizational, and Human Resource Questions

- Contract, Tax, Regulatory, and Processes and Controls Questions

Many questions point to the heart of value—the certainty and resiliency of future cash flows. Some cover issues that are not deal-breakers but could slow a deal down, introducing additional risk to closing the transaction. Taken as a whole, the questions help to build a picture of a professionally managed company that is ready for growth.

What Do You Want to Achieve by Selling Your Business?

There is no wrong answer to the question above, as long as the answer is your truth. So before you initiate the sales process, do some soul-searching to determine your primary goals for selling the business.

This process of clarifying your values is a key to success. It will help inform you regarding the types of advisors you need as you look for buyers. It may also help determine the most likely buyers of your business, the terms you are willing to accept, and other elements of the process itself.

While it may seem obvious that the goal of selling your business is to maximize the amount of after-tax cash proceeds you receive at closing and then walk away, many owners find that they have other goals that are equally important.

You should strive to maximize the value of your company for the type of transaction you want to do.

If your goal is to achieve the absolute maximum value and walk away from the business within a relatively short period, say 180 days, then you will most likely want to hire an investment banker with strong experience in both your industry and expected deal size. They will probably conduct a full-blown auction that will entail marketing the company to a wide variety of buyers, including international buyers. This type of process and transaction creates the most competition and therefore should determine the maximum value of your company. In such an auction, potential buyers may be willing to pay a premium price to achieve their strategic goals. Those goals might include entering a new product and service market, moving into a new geographic area with an established customer base, or removing a competitor from the market.

However, an auction process usually introduces the highest risk of major disruption to your management team and employee base. It could result in moving the company's operations to another location, even an international location. It could result in significant cuts to the senior and middle management team and complete elimination of back-office functions and staff.

It may seem heartless to pursue a maximum payout given the potential disruption to the business and to the colleagues who have helped you build it. However, there are many businesses in which the owner has had to continually reinvest the profits of the business into growth and research and development. Other owners have chosen to keep most of the business's earnings on the company's balance sheet to avoid debt or to maintain a rainy-day fund to cushion against inevitable downturns in the economy. These owners only get one payday: the day they sell their business. For them, maximization of value is an understandable goal.

For other owners, income from their business has been strong for years, and they may be willing to accept less than maximum value for their business to accomplish some alternative goals. For some of these owners, leaving the business and its name intact as a major local employer and community supporter is an important legacy. For others, selling to new owners who have a history of keeping existing management teams in place is vital. Finally, some owners are willing to forgo a big payday at the closing to enable existing management or their children to purchase the business over time, often five to twenty years.

For example, during my consulting career we were once called in to advise a business owner regarding an offer he had received from an investment group. The offer was $55 million for 100 percent of the company. We advised our client that our research into the current valuations of companies in the same industry and similar in size indicated his company's value could be at least 15 percent higher than the offer.

He stated that he knew that was probably the case but that these potential buyers had committed to leaving the company in its current location and, except for his replacement, retaining the management team. Because the business was one of the largest employers in his smaller city in the South and because he had been receiving large distributions from the company for years, he was willing to consider a lower price in exchange for less disruption to his company and employees. He would also avoid a longer, more disruptive sale process than if he set up an auction to create the competition necessary to maximize the sales price.

Other owners may wish to recommit themselves to taking their businesses to the next level of growth and profitability but at the same time need to secure their long-term financial future and diversify their personal wealth so that all their net worth is not tied up in the business.

These owners may need to find a financial buyer such as a private equity firm to purchase 60 percent to 90 percent of the business, securing their retirement but also providing capital to rapidly expand the company. In this scenario, the owner lowers the risk on his personal balance sheet, gets the opportunity to lead the company to a new level one last time, and hopefully enjoys a second significant liquidity event (i.e., a second large payday when their remaining ownership in the business is sold).

The scenarios are virtually unlimited, but the key is to determine what outcomes are most important to you.

55 Questions
To Ask Before You
Sell Your Business

General Financial Questions to Ask Before You Sell Your Business

1.

Are My Financial Records in Tip-Top Shape?

Nothing erodes a potential buyer's confidence—and therefore the value of your business—faster than messy and disorganized financial records.

Most transactions evolve as follows: the seller provides financial statements to the buyer along with some additional general operational data, a value and deal structure are agreed upon and documented via a non-binding letter of intent, and then the buyer begins the due diligence process.

If buyers sense the financial records are inaccurate, do not reflect sound accounting practices, or are clearly not useful for managing the business and making decisions, it is likely you will never receive an offer.

In fact, most potential buyers, particularly financial professionals such as private equity firms and investment bankers but also corporate development departments of larger organizations, have many deals to review and look for quick ways to eliminate deals. If your financials are messy and hard to explain, you have made it easy for them to toss your deal and move on to something easier and more understandable. Most will not go to the trouble of reconstructing your financials to help you out.

An even worse scenario than getting eliminated from the stack before an offer is made is receiving and accepting an offer from a buyer and then moving into due diligence with unreliable financial records. As already stated, once a deal is struck, value almost always moves only one direction: down.

The answer to this issue is to invest in qualified internal or external resources to improve the quality and timeliness of your financial records. Our consulting firm has built an entire professional services practice around helping smaller and lower middle market companies improve the quality of their financial statements by providing fractional chief financial officer and controller services to aid client staff or by providing a fully outsourced accounting solution.

We routinely enter new client relationships because the company needs to access more capital, usually through bank borrowing, or has received an offer to be acquired. Almost without exception, we discover that the financial records are in much worse condition than ownership or management believes, and the company routinely incurs professional fees two to three times the cost of qualified annual accounting costs to clean up the mess. And of course, in this scenario management must clean up the mess while the banker or potential suitor waits, often not too patiently.

Regardless of how you choose to address this issue, there is a tangible payoff even before you are in the process of selling your business. Well-organized records will give your banker more confidence in the quality of your financial statements, resulting in expanded lines of credit or lower cost of borrowing. And when it comes time to sell your business, potential buyers will have confidence that your records represent a true picture of your financial success.

2.

Should I Invest in an Independent Audit of My Financial Statements?

Yes.

That may not be a surprising answer from a partner in a certified public accounting firm that earns 40 percent of its revenue from audit services, but I have spent most of my career on the other side of the table, working as a CFO and buying companies. The purpose of audited financial statements is to provide assurance to the reader that the company's financial statements are fairly stated and free from material errors. In return, the company receives greater access to capital at a lower cost than if it did not have audited financial statements.

This access to capital is not limited only to growth capital in the form of bank debt and public capital markets. It also includes access to capital in the form of capital for a buyer purchasing the equity or the assets of your company.

That is not just a theory. In the realm of small, lower middle market, and middle market companies, businesses with financial statements audited by a CPA firm that is respected in your industry and/or geographic region is a true differentiator.

Listed below are a few of the ways investing in audited financial statements will benefit you during a transaction:

- Increase the population of potential suitors. Again, professional buyers are often looking for ways to eliminate deals from their list of options to evaluate. Businesses without audited financial statements may be eliminated first or moved to the bottom of the stack in hopes the buyer finds an easier, more compelling deal.

- Confirm your revenue recognition and expensing policies. An audit will ensure that your policies for recognizing revenues and accruing expenses are solidly within the guidelines of generally accepted accounting principles in the United States (GAAP). It will also ensure that industry- or company-specific accounting issues are being handled correctly. Finding out your financial statements are not being presented in accordance with GAAP during the due diligence process often results in material adjustments to the purchase price. In some instances, this realization may become an insurmountable hurdle to the transaction.

- Create or improve your system of internal controls. A financial audit conducted by an independent CPA firm is not designed to detect fraud or provide assurance as to the efficacy of your internal controls, but the auditor is required to review the system of internal controls and bring to your attention any material deficiencies in your system of internal controls as they relate to the fair presentation of the financial statements. It is true, of course, that many smaller or non-complex companies have difficulty segregating accounting duties enough to create a robust system of internal controls. However, investing in an annual audit will help you identify and mitigate significant control weaknesses and provide valuable peace of mind to both you and potential buyers.

- Change the starting point of due diligence in a deal. With at least two years of audited financial statements in hand when a deal is struck, you can be assured that the buyer will enter the due diligence process with confidence. High-quality financial information makes a more accurate foundation for determining your business's value.

- The audit process prepares your team for financial due diligence. The financial due diligence process has many similarities to the annual audit process. In both, there are reconciliations to perform, schedules to prepare, and many questions to answer. Engaging in an annual audit will prepare your accounting team for the due diligence process.

The annual audit process is expensive. The professional fees for an audit of a small to mid-sized firm typically range from $30,000 to $100,000 or more, depending on the complexity of the business. Given this cost, it is understandable why owners try to avoid an audit unless their bankers, industry regulations, or investors require it.

It is difficult if not impossible to determine if audited financial statements increase final transaction value, but I stand by the assertions above, plus one more: audited financial statements have a material bearing on the most important factor in any transaction—that it closes.

3.

Do I Mix Personal Expenses in My Business Records?

The primary purpose of the financial due diligence process is to determine the true cash flows of the operations of the business. To do this requires "normalizing" the cash flows being generated by the business.

In the normalizing process, the company's net income is adjusted to "add-back" discretionary and personal expenses paid by the company on the owner's behalf to arrive at the cash flows derived solely from company operations. The result of these adjustments are typically called "normalized EBITDA," earnings before interest, taxes, depreciation, and amortization, in transaction jargon. (Note there are many other types of normalization adjustments that might come into play in the process of normalizing cash flows, but this discussion is limited to discretionary and personal expenses.) See Appendix A for an example of this calculation.

In proper accounting, purely personal expenses paid by the company should be recorded as distributions to the owners. However, there is significant judgment involved in defining a legitimate tax-deductible business expense, so some business owners flirt with (or fly right over) the line that separates legitimate from illegitimate tax-deductible expenses. The slang for this loose accounting treatment is FAAP (family accepted accounting principles). While FAAP is not GAAP, buyers are generally not going to spend a lot of time passing judgment on your decisions in this regard. The primary issue is to get to the true cash flows of the operations of the company.

As this process unfolds, you will be working diligently to identify all the discretionary and personal expenses that can legitimately be added back to net income or EBITDA to strengthen your operating cash flows. Many transactions are valued based on a multiple of EBITA, say, five to seven times EBITA, so there is a strong incentive to identify as many add-backs as possible to potentially drive the purchase price higher. Simply put, on a valuation of five times EBITDA, every add-back dollar identified could potentially put $5 more in your pocket. An additional $100,000 in add-backs translates to $500,000 in additional purchase price. It adds up in a hurry.

Given those stakes, the add-backs typically receive a lot of attention in the buyer's due diligence process. The buyer will want solid backup in the form of invoices, payroll records, and other source documents to verify the legitimacy of these add-backs. The process of providing that documentation can be tedious and time-consuming, and depending on the expenses that have been claimed, it can begin to feel like an invasion of privacy.

We recommend owners avoid as many of these expenses as possible, particularly the personal expenses that are in the gray area of tax deductibility, starting three years or more out from a planned transaction. Doing so will simplify the reconciliation between reported net income or EBITDA and "normalized EBITDA."

It is hard to quantify the value of creating a stronger separation between business and personal expenses, but one of the impacts will be less time and effort scrutinizing and questioning these expenses. And shortening the time spent in due diligence is always valuable to the seller, usually with the reward of a higher likelihood of closing the transaction.

4.

Does My Monthly Accounting Closing Process Ensure Financial Statements Are Accurate?

One of the primary ways to drive confidence into the buyer's perception of your company, and particularly your company's financial reporting, is to develop and follow a solid monthly accounting closing process.

The typical acquisition takes 90 to 180 days to complete from letter of intent to closing. During this period, the buyer will want to see monthly updates on the company's financial performance to ensure the business is meeting expectations. In many smaller companies, there is often a lack of emphasis on closing the books with both a sense of urgency and accuracy. If your closing process is nonexistent or takes more than thirty days to accomplish, the buyer will be left wondering how the business is doing as the closing draws near.

In our practice, we see two extremes. Most commonly, the books are left open for thirty days or more so that every vendor invoice that comes in for the last month can be recorded. This practice results in a 100 percent accurate portrayal of expenses, but since another full month has elapsed, the records' usefulness for decision making has passed.

A less frequent scenario is that the books are closed on the final day of the month or a day or two later, without regard to whether all the expenses from the previous month have been recorded. This approach allows the company to print financial statements within a day or two of month's end. However, these statements are usually inaccurate and result in lumpy month-to-month results that do not accurately reflect company operations in any given month.

The monthly closing process should emphasize proper matching of revenues and expenses. Revenue recognition is one of the most challenging aspects of GAAP accounting, and in many business models and industries there is a time lapse between proper revenue recognition and customer billings. Some companies find it difficult to grapple with this lapse, along with other aspects of accrual accounting. Companies can overcome these issues by investing in stronger accounting talent and good processes.

The benefits of these improvements will be monthly financial statements that accurately tell the story of your business's financial condition. Potential buyers' confidence erodes during the due diligence process if you are constantly explaining that one month's results were overstated because certain transactions were not recorded until the next month and the following month's results were understated because they included expenses from the month before.

This issue would be unlikely to kill a deal, but it could extend the due diligence process and generate more and more questions, which is never to your benefit as a seller.

This issue has an easy fix. Invest in a qualified, experienced accounting controller and set expectations to close the books accurately within seven to ten workdays each month.

5.

Have I Promised Remuneration to Key Employees if I Ever Sell the Business?

"I'm going to take care of you if I ever sell this business."

"Thanks for sticking with me through that rough patch the last two years. If I ever sell this business, I'll make sure you get at least 10 percent of the pie."

"I could not do this without you. When I sell this thing, I'll see to it that you are taken care of."

Sound familiar?

As a business owner, you rely heavily on a few key people who help drive your company's success. It is natural to want to reward them when the day comes to monetize the value of the business you have built.

We have seen many instances when owners have made oral, email, or texted promises like those above to key individuals, sometimes in the heat of a crisis. You meant the promises when you made them and want to fulfill them, but all too often these intentions are never put into a formal agreement and are left open until a transaction is on the table and your key employee is standing in your office reminding you of your promises.

Once a deal is on the table and you are trying to fulfill your promises, several problems may come into extreme focus:

- You may have a very different definition of "take care of" than your key employee does.

- The employee may have a valid and enforceable claim even though he now works at your competitor.

- You may not be able to realize the level of after-tax net proceeds you expected when you made the promise, so your ability and willingness to share in the proceeds may have changed.

- You find that the time has long passed for any possibility of the proceeds to be paid to the employee to be taxed at capital gains rates.

Promises to involve employees in the results of a sale need to be set in writing. You can structure these agreements as tax-effective retention tools while still maintaining full control of the organization, but those issues are beyond the scope of this book.

Owners often avoid setting these promises in writing for a variety of reasons, but you can be assured that your key employees will not forget them. When a transaction is on the table, you will need your employees like never before. They will be essential to helping you sell the deal to the employee base and ensuring as smooth a transition as possible to the new owner.

Similarly, owners should consider various estate planning and gifting scenarios as early as possible in the evolution of the business toward its eventual sale. Like providing proceeds to key employees, proceeds can be transferred in a tax-efficient way to children, spouses, and charities if planned well in advance, especially while the company's fair value is relatively low compared to the hoped-for eventual transaction value. Consult with appropriate legal and accounting advisors who specialize in estate and wealth transfer planning to understand the various alternatives available to you along with the pros and cons of each alternative.

6.

Do I Routinely Cull Customers Who Place Unreasonable Demands on Our Organization?

Do you have customers you wish would do business with your competitors?

They place unreasonable delivery demands on your production schedule, they are never happy with your services, they always want a lower price, and they routinely abuse your employees.

If you are not already in the habit of firing these abusive customers, then planning a sale of your business in the next one to three years needs to be catalyst for you to do so.

Why?

Because in most smaller and lower middle market transactions, the current owner (i.e., the seller) has a vested financial interest in the future success of the company and should do everything possible to increase the likelihood of that success.

Many transactions include earn-outs or seller notes. They may also require the seller to roll over some level of equity and remain engaged in their company at some level. Earn-outs are typically used to bridge the gap between the seller's and buyer's valuation expectations. In a common example, the seller receives a certain amount of the purchase price in cash at closing plus additional purchase consideration a few years in the future if certain criteria, such as a revenue goal or EBITDA growth rate, are met.

Seller notes are often used when the business is "asset light," as is typical for most service-oriented businesses. In this scenario, the buyer's ability to secure traditional bank financing is limited due to the lack of hard assets (such as buildings, equipment, and inventory) to collateralize a loan. The seller agrees to finance the remaining portion of the transaction proceeds through a note payable (a promise from the buyer to pay in the future). This seller note is subordinated in priority to the bank's position, meaning if the business is struggling under the management of the buyer, the bank has a right to be paid first.

In an equity rollover, the seller is required to reinvest a portion of the proceeds back into the company at the transaction valuation. This requirement keeps the seller engaged in the company and sets him on equal footing with the new owner in terms of invested capital per ownership interest.

In all of these deal structures, a portion of the seller's ultimate consideration depends on the future success of the company.

Therefore, after closing, all parties need to be laser focused on maintaining and increasing the profitability of the business. If instead the new owners or you are distracted by toxic customers, then those future results could be in jeopardy.

Firing abusive customers is not easy, but the benefits have been proven again and again across many different business models and industries.

The profile of your customer list most likely reflects the Pareto principle, more commonly known as the 80/20 rule. In short, you should expect that 80 percent of your total profits come from 20 percent of your customers. Conversely, the remaining 20 percent of profits come from 80 percent of your customers. It should not be a shock that your toxic customers fall into this latter category. Furthermore, it also likely that you spend 80 percent of your customer service time trying to keep these toxic customers happy.

You may be hesitant to fire any customers lest you devalue your company's cash flows and therefore potential transaction value. Starting the culling process well ahead of an anticipated transaction will mitigate that risk.

When you analyze your most toxic customers, you may find that you lose money on them because of all the extra time and attention it takes to please them. In that scenario, your cash flows will increase if you fire them—even if revenues go down. Further, if you start this process three years in advance, you will have ample time to replace these customers with fewer, more profitable relationships, enhancing transaction value in the long term.

When it comes to positioning your company for post-closing success, culling troublesome customers is good for business.

Revenue and Profitability Questions to Ask Before You Sell Your Business

7.

How Predictable Are My Revenues and Gross Profits?

Predictability is the cornerstone of building confidence in future results. And in a possible transaction, confidence translates into increased valuation and higher likelihood of closing.

Given the stakes, it is worth your effort to try to fully understand where your operating results are predictable and where they are not. For the less predictable elements, you may be able to discern patterns and relationships that will help to increase confidence in future results.

Some business models and industries—typically mature industries with stable pricing levels and steady growth trends—produce inherently consistent and therefore predictable revenues and gross profits. Other business models, however, such as custom manufacturers who fabricate, ship, and install large orders, produce lumpy results. In these businesses, the timing of revenue recognition is triggered by shipping patterns, which may be irregular, and gross margins may vary widely by customer or product line.

I encourage you to dive deep into your revenues and gross profits to identify trends and patterns in your own business model.

For example, many equipment manufacturers may state that their replacement parts sales have no rhyme or reason. "Some months are great; some months are weak." However, upon further investigation, they may find that customers' maintenance programs operate seasonally and that replacement parts orders follow suit. Alternatively, parts orders may be highly affected by inside sales efforts. Or there may be a strong correlation between the age of their main products and the sale of replacement parts.

In the technology company I served as CFO, we determined that more than one-third of our break/fix revenues were derived from a few southeastern states, with most of those revenues earned from April through July, when strong pop-up storms with heavy lightning rolled through on hot afternoons. This realization allowed us to better forecast earnings from a part of our business we had previously considered completely unpredictable.

Your deep dive will likely require experimenting with analysis of different segments such as product lines, equipment versus services revenues streams, customer sets, geographical locations, or seasons. The commonalities and predictabilities you can discern in your operational and financial records will help build prospective buyers' confidence about future results.

8.

Do I Have a High Concentration of Revenues With a Few Key Customers?

Customer concentration is a big red flag to most prospective buyers. You probably already have a sense of this issue from working with your banker, who also does not want your ability to repay debt to be dependent on few customer relationships.

In an article on InvestmentBank.com, Nate Nead, a principal at Deal Capital Partners, LLC states it this way: "Regardless of the model, the product or the service being offered, every target becomes more inviting when the customer base is diversified. I'll say it again differently and perhaps more clearly, a diversified customer base can significantly increase your business valuation."

When ownership of a business changes, all relationships, especially customer relationships, are at risk. Prospective buyers factor this reality into the value they are willing to pay for the business. These relationship risks include 1) the new ownership may be unable to retain key customers; 2) key customers may use the transaction as an excuse to shop their business to competitors; and 3) key customers may use the transaction and your dependence on them as leverage to extract price or other costly concessions from you. These are real concerns, and they can severely damage the buyer's transaction economics.

There are many definitions of customer concentration, but in general revenues are considered concentrated once one to three customers account for more than 20 percent of your revenues.

If customer concentration is an issue in your business, what can you do in the planning stages of a transaction to try to mitigate the risk?

- Determine if your customer base is truly concentrated. The risks around customer concentration are primarily about the customer's buying channels. Carefully analyze and document how your customers interact with you and their other vendors before you accept the notion your business has customer concentration issues.

  For example, a client we've worked with intermittently for several years engaged us to conduct pre-sale, sell-side due diligence to give them an idea of an approximate transaction value and how they would fare in the due diligence process. At the outset of the project, they stated that customer concentration was an issue because there are only four major manufacturers of the products they work with.

  However, we found that each of these manufacturers divided their U.S. market into four regions, each of which was a separately managed buying channel, and that major metropolitan areas within each region also operated as separate buying channels. Finally, we discovered our client's customers also included other professional designers and industry consultants who recommended their products. In all, we identified more than two hundred unique relationships that the company was managing within the boundaries of those four customers.

  If this company ever embarks on a sales process, they will now be able to counter the "customer concentration" argument with real data.

- Develop multiple relationships at each key customer to mitigate the risk of concentration. Develop a customer service plan for each major customer that involves developing relationships with employees both above and below your buyer within the organization. For example, try to develop peer-to-peer relationships between functional leaders (in sales, operations, and finance) at both organizations, including with the customer's CEO or owner. Other ways to broaden the relationship might include initiating a vendor review process and insisting on a broader audience at the meeting, inviting key customer personnel to a hospitality suite during an industry trade show or conference, or developing a product or services roadmap presentation and inviting a broad audience from the customer.

The key is to establish deep connections at the customer and do everything in your power to prevent the primary contact from controlling your access to other key decision-makers. If your company's relationship with major customers is limited to a single person, such as the procurement officer, that should be a red flag that the relationship has significant risk to you now— not just in a potential acquisition. Likewise, if your relationship with the customer is controlled by just one person on your team, that is also a red flag that needs to be addressed (see Question 10).

- Diversify the customer base. Expanding a customer base is always much easier said than done. In the typical case of a company that has significant customer concentration issues, the company has shaped their entire organization, from quoting to product and service options to field service and to billing, around pleasing its major customers. As a result, the procedures that keep this relationship secure are the same procedures that make it difficult to secure other major accounts.

The most efficient approach to diversifying a customer base is to focus your efforts on current customers who should be buying more goods and services from you. This approach is usually much more productive and faster than starting a new relationship from scratch, although some effort needs to be applied to gaining new customers as well.

In efforts to grow the customer base, your direct involvement is necessary for success. Talk about the importance of this initiative, meet with key customers and prospects, and consistently follow up on action items. If you don't signal to the organization that change must happen, the team will drift back to what is comfortable, which is making the big customer happy.

Finally, in some industries or market niches, customer concentration is a reality. While efforts to mitigate the risk should be undertaken, it may not be possible to eliminate those risks entirely. If this is true for your business, know that companies with heavy customer concentrations can be sold. In fact, we have seen several single-customer companies sell. In these instances, buyers typically discount their purchase price compared to a similar business with a well-diversified customer base and negotiate for additional support from the owner to ensure a successful transition of the customer base. Usually, the buyer secures this post-closing support from the exiting owner by making a portion of the purchase price contingent upon the successful transition of the customer to the new owner.

In summary, diversifying your customer base will help reduce risk to potential acquirers, thereby giving you, the selling owner, additional pricing power in a transaction negotiation. However, if customer concentration is an issue, do what you can to mitigate this risk and understand you may have to support the transaction by conceding some value or deferring the proceeds until the buyer is confident the customer relationship has transitioned successfully.

9.

Am I the Key Customer Contact for My Business?

If you control all your business's key customer relationships, you have created a risk to a possible sale. Prospective buyers will naturally worry that when you leave the business, the customers will leave as well—or at least consider their options.

The biggest hindrance to transitioning customer relationships to others in your organization is usually pushback from the customers themselves. They like the fact that they deal directly with the owner. If they need a favor, they can call you direct and get an answer quickly. There are no gatekeepers. They are talking directly to the main decision-maker.

Most customers want to be treated as special and have their needs met promptly. The number one way to help a customer transition to someone besides you is for your designee to give them better service and responsiveness than they receive from you. That will take a strong effort from your designee, as well as some strategically slower responses from you over time.

As in companies with customer concentration issues, for owners who fail to transition customer relationships before selling their business, deal terms may require that a portion of the purchase price is not released until after a successful transition of key customer relationships. While not ideal for the seller, this alternative is usually better than an outright discount of the purchase price, and it's certainly better than no deal at all.

10.

Is My Business Beholden to One Key Salesperson?

If a single salesperson controls all or most of your major accounts, you're facing the customer concentration issue in reverse. However, prospective buyers view this situation as less risky than customer concentration because there are several ways to deal with it in the transaction.

Even so, it is not healthy for your business to have too many relationships tied up in one key salesperson. If the goal is to remove as many obstacles as possible before a potential transaction, your salesperson concentration needs to be addressed.

Realize that in many cases, customers are not as tied to their salesperson as you may assume. If your business has service personnel who are installing or maintaining your products or if you have service providers who are executing the scope of work separately from the salesperson, your customer likely puts much more emphasis on their relationship with these individuals than on their relationship with their salesperson, even if he or she is the one who delivers donuts to their office every week. Notwithstanding all the cheers from the customer's office staff, donuts do not outweigh outstanding customer service when it comes time to measure relationship quality.

You can use the same peer-to-peer effort as discussed in Question 8. Creating relationships between customers and personnel throughout your organization is healthy and beneficial, whether you sell your business soon or not.

A final mitigating tactic to alleviate salesperson concentration is to require all salespeople to sign non-solicit agreements when you hire them. You should not freelance this issue. Get qualified legal counsel to draft an agreement that is effective and enforceable in your state. As with any contract, there must be consideration given for it to be enforceable. If you require the non-solicit agreement to be executed at the time of employment, then that will count as consideration given by the company in most states. It is much harder to prove consideration after employment has been established and in place for any period of time, but a qualified attorney who practices in employment law can guide you.

In my experience, customers do not move their business with their salesperson as quickly and easily as most sales professionals would have you believe. However, it is still a risk worth addressing by maintaining competitive compensation plans and supporting high performing salespersons with solid administrative and operational resources to allow them to consistently execute at a high level. Taking care of these high performers and implementing a few appropriate risk-mitigation strategies will greatly alleviate the prospective buyers' concerns about salesperson concentration.

11.

Does My Business Have a Strong Source of Recurring Revenues?

Recurring revenues. The sweetest words in business.

All other things being equal, businesses with multiyear or evergreen customer contracts that require fixed recurring payments drive the highest valuations. In fact, in many industries where the dominant business model is monthly recurring revenues, transactions are valued based on a multiple of monthly recurring revenues rather than on the more common approach of a multiple of EBITDA. The most frequently cited examples of these business models are home alarm businesses, software-as-a-service companies, and subscription-based offerings such as for meals or movies.

Recurring revenues are almost always more valuable than other revenues because they typically drive higher gross profit margins. With a steady stream of reliable revenues, businesses can create efficient and effective processes to deliver their products or services. Recurring revenues also create consistent and predictable cash flows, which simplifies cash management and usually reduces costs of billing and collection.

For example, we once worked with a client whose business was overhauling turbo prop airplane engines, an expense of $250,000 to $400,000 for the operator of the aircraft. Under the traditional model, the aircraft operators had to either diligently set aside funds for this expense or borrow money and repay it after the overhaul was completed.

This approach created a cash flow burden for the aircraft operator and a collection risk for our client. Our client created a pay-by-the-mile program in which the aircraft owner paid a small fee for each hour the engine was operated. The fee was structured such that when the engine needed an overhaul, the cost was completely covered. Since most of his customers earn revenues based on the aircraft's operating hours, the program matches the cost of the overhaul with their cash inflows.

Additionally, the cost of the overhaul can be discounted for customers on the pay-by-the-mile program since there is no collection risk and our client can plan his shop maintenance schedule months in advance. In addition to these benefits, this client will enjoy an enhanced valuation when the time comes to market the company to potential buyers.

Some businesses have a good base of recurring revenues but may not realize it. The most common definition of monthly recurring revenues is a contractual agreement with a customer to pay a fixed monthly fee for a product or service. However, if a business can demonstrate that certain customers purchase relatively consistent amounts each month, quarter, or year (and have for several years), then these patterns should be documented and can be presented as a form of recurring revenues.

The technology company I worked for had a strong base of contracted recurring revenues through maintenance contracts on various telecommunications devices. However, not all equipment malfunctions were covered under the maintenance contract. After accumulating and analyzing several years of data, we determined that our break/fix revenues consistently averaged 20 percent of our monthly contract revenues, except in those months when these revenues spiked due to strong electrical storms in the southeastern United States. By documenting this relationship and continuing to monitor it, we were comfortable including these revenues in our calculation of recurring revenues when discussing results with analysts as well as when we were marketing the company for sale.

It is well worth your time to identify all the recurring revenue in your business. Doing so could dramatically change the valuation of your company.

12.

Do I Have Good Data to Support My Decisions?

You have run your business for years. You know its rhythms and have a gut feeling for how things are going because you sign the checks, fund the payroll, and stroll through the shop floor or warehouse.

Prospective buyers will not have your experience. They will need data—not just to eventually run the business, but to evaluate it during the sales process.

This point was driven home a few years ago when we were working with an owner who ran a large parking facility that also provided an airport shuttle service. He wanted to attract additional capital to his business to fund expansion to a new location, a process not too different from the sales process.

During our initial conversations, we began to investigate the data he used to make decisions on staffing, shuttle schedules, and pricing. Specifically, we asked about car counts. His initial response was that he looked out the window every morning to see how full the lot was. This was a perfectly legitimate answer from an owner who had been operating an airport parking facility for more than thirty years. In addition to having a gut feeling for the number of cars in his lot, he knew all the key arrival and departure times of the airlines, and he knew the ebbs and flows of customer demand throughout each day of the week.

Unfortunately, a prospective new owner, or in his case a potential investor or lender, would not inherently know those data points. Potential investors need to be assured this data is accumulated accurately and reliably and can be presented in a meaningful format.

If your business does not have adequate reporting systems to collect financial and operational data, develop those systems and processes well ahead of the sales process so prospective buyers will be able to review meaningful historical data. Buyers know that you rely heavily on your experience and even your gut, but presenting data that supports your decisions and that can be translated into demonstrated financial results is a powerful tool to drive buyer confidence.

As noted in Question 1, the starting point is reliable, relevant, and timely financial statements. As advisors who specialize in accounting and in developing financial reporting systems for owners, we are continually amazed at the number of business owners who have built substantial and successful businesses but have chosen not to invest in the proper resources for financial reporting.

These owners typically use customized spreadsheets to monitor project status or manufacturing outputs that bear no relationship to the results reflected in their accounting system. They use their accounting system and staff like a checkbook—to pay vendors and employees and prepare customer invoices. All the meaningful information used to make decisions and measure progress and results is maintained in these customized spreadsheets. While this disjointed process works for the current owner, a prospective buyer, particularly one that would like to grow the business quickly, will value systems that produce accurate results that are reflected in the financial statements.

In addition to financial systems, you should also consider systems that collect and report operational data. Examples of this data include direct and indirect labor hours, machine hours, units produced, service tickets initiated and resolved, and materials yield. Various operational systems may already collect this data, but it should be analyzed in context with financial records as well.

These kinds of investments, both in systems and in the staff to operate and maintain them, can seem overwhelming and costly to business owners. It is always important to moderate the investment against the value derived. However, businesses that make investments in these tools commensurate with their size, complexity, and future growth expectations will be rewarded in the sales process with a high level of interest, strong confidence, and possibly higher valuation.

The highest valuations are paid to companies that have systems already positioned for transformative growth. These companies receive a premium from buyers who want to rapidly consolidate an industry from a strong foundation. Why shouldn't that company be yours?

13.

Is My Procurement Process Reliant on My Day-to-Day Involvement?

Many business owners rightly understand that much of their success and profitability is directly related to their company's success in the procurement process.

We have had the opportunity to work with many engineering firms over the years. In our experience, engineers have one of two approaches to procurement: 1) They view procurement as an ancillary service some customers require to shift the risk of purchasing the appropriate equipment (to the engineer rather than the customer. 2) They view procurement as an opportunity to drive customer value and satisfaction into a transaction and to bring additional profit to the engineering firm.

The former engineers resist taking on the responsibility of procurement at every turn and only accept it if it is a requirement to win the engineering work. This group passes along procured equipment at modest markups of 5 to 10 percent to cover the cost and hassle of executing the procurement transaction.

The latter engineers look for opportunities to exercise their procurement prowess. They sell the customer on the concept of off-loading the burden of purchasing from the customer's already overworked staff. The more risk-tolerant engineers in this group take an even more aggressive posture by bundling their services, both engineering and equipment, into a full turn-key, fixed-price solution. Then, in the background, these engineers work with equipment suppliers and fabricators to drive down costs and increase efficiencies for both parties, resulting in competitive but more profitable pricing. These engineers are rewarded with substantially increased profitability by strategically accepting the additional risk of procurement.

Even if you are not the owner of an engineering firm, you probably understand the value proposition of procurement and its impact on profitability.

Progressive businesses are developing vendor management programs that drive process and win-win relationships with key suppliers. In these initiatives, companies come together with vendors for the long-haul. Key aspects of most vendor management programs are:

- Agreed rules of engagement to define business practices and ethical principles;

- An understanding of each company's business model and what drives value so that win-win relationships can be built;

- Agreement on terms, conditions, and production or delivery schedules;

- Integration of systems to reduce communications errors and labor costs of inputting, tracking, and reporting data;

- Performance monitoring through periodic reviews in which both sides honestly assess what is working and what needs improvement; and

- Regular renewals and reassessments to ensure contracts, pricing, and terms are up to date.

By encouraging your team's broader involvement in procurement, you remove yourself from the central position in the process, reduce the risk of an individual becoming too cozy with a supplier, and create scalability in a key part of your business.

Prospective buyers will value a professional approach to procurement that is more easily transitioned to a new owner.

14.

Do I Have an Effective Process to Quote New Business?

As we have established, most transactions are valued on a multiple of EBITDA basis, and companies that are well run and positioned for high growth receive a premium valuation compared to other market participants.

We constantly see good companies experiencing mediocre financial results year after year. When we look into the reasons, we often find one or two dud jobs that occur nearly every year. The company proposed, won, and executed dozens of projects efficiently and hit their expected profit margins. But there was one project, often a larger-than-average one, that went south. Often, these poorly performing jobs could have been prevented with a more effective quoting process. As a result, annual results are hurt, and historical EBITDA is diminished, thereby reducing the business valuation. You may argue effectively that a single poorly performed job should be adjusted out of your results, but if it is a recurring event, as it often is, you are not likely to win that argument.

We also often see companies that do not have a structured process for quoting new work. Each salesperson uses their own template, produces a unique deliverable to the customer, and is responsible for the quote's quality and accuracy. If you are skeptical about accuracy being a problem, I would simply offer up the oft-quoted statistic that 88 percent of spreadsheets contain a mathematical error.

Although this scenario allows for creativity and freedom for the sales staff, it is not a scalable process, does not manage the inherent risk in quoting projects, and does not support a consistent company brand. A better system would result in a consistent look and feel for customer deliverables and enable new sales personnel or newly acquired companies to be integrated more easily.

To improve quality and consistency in the quoting process and to create a platform for growth in this functional area of your business, consider these criteria:

- The same quoting tool should be used across the entire company, or at least by major product or service line.

- Complete customer data, including delivery location and contact, billing location and contact, and any special tax considerations, should be collected as part of the quoting process.

- A clearly worded scope should be stated on the quote using language common in your industry.

- The parts and services items quoted should be identical in both number and description to listings in your company's inventory and accounting systems.

- The quoting tool should have up-to-date cost information for materials and labor, and there should be controls in place to prevent the use of outdated cost data.

- The quoting tool should have a defined process for including overhead costs.

- The quoting tool should have built-in logic that identifies product and service dependencies—for example, if you order Item X, you must also include Item Y.

- The quoting tool should have built-in minimum profit margins and should require management approval to override those minimums.

- The quoting tool should require larger project quotes to be reviewed by key management or a specialized team to ensure quality and accuracy.

- The process should include a prompt review after large projects are completed to compare the original quote to the actual results.

Speed is always important in the quoting process, so whenever possible, automate these elements, particularly those that tie back to key databases such as parts and services lists and pricing and cost data.

The quoting process is like an archer letting go of his arrow. With great aim, he hits the mark, but if he is off just a fraction, he misses the target. Too often in business, we rush to win a deal and hope our execution teams can overcome our poor aim. Usually, this results in increased labor costs, incorrect parts orders, redoing work, return trips to the customer location, and unmet schedules.

A good process can fix these issues and mitigate the risk of those annual dud jobs that must be explained to a prospective buyer and dampen valuations.

15.

Are My Prices and Service Rates Updated Consistently to Reflect Changing Market Conditions?

When a business transitions to new ownership, the first thing customers want to know is whether their pricing will change. This is especially true for services businesses. When the acquired company has not kept its pricing consistent with market rates or has not raised prices in several years, the buyer may perceive an increased risk that the customer base will erode soon after the acquisition. The more risk the prospective buyer perceives, the more they will discount the value of your business.

Maintaining a healthy pricing posture sends many positive signals about your business. Regular price adjustments indicate:

- You deliver high value to customers and are willing to commit to continuing to improve that value over time.

- You are committed to recruiting, training, and retaining great people to serve your customers.

- You are committed to investing in technology, research and development, and good processes to improve the customer's experience.

- You value the talents and abilities of the people who work for you and are not willing to give their efforts away at a sub-market rate.

- You believe your goods and services are commensurate in value with those of the market leaders in your industry or geographic area.

Of course, you must deliver on those commitments for customers to experience and value them.

A few years ago, while conducting due diligence for a client on a potential acquisition target, we inquired about the pricing of the target's professional services, which was significantly below market rates. The target's owner bragged that his customers loved his company and that he could raise their rates without any problem. It begged the question, "Who is stopping you?"

This target company produced an outstanding product. But by not instituting a price change in several years, the owner had inadvertently positioned himself as a high-quality but cheap service provider. Naturally, he had plenty of business. But he also did not have competitive salaries, benefits, and training programs, so his growth was largely constrained to his current workforce. His inability to grow was a major factor in his decision to market his business, and he was not in a position of strength entering the negotiations.

Our client's primary strategy was to use the target's services as an internal resource to create more capacity to quote and execute business and to bundle these services into a much larger sale. Therefore, the target's pricing issues were less relevant. Most other buyers, however, would have needed to factor in the time and risk associated with raising prices, knowing it would take several years and probably a few customer losses to bring the target's pricing up to market levels. Most likely, these buyers would discount their valuation of the target to accept these risks.

Regular evaluation of your pricing will force you to think through your value proposition, which will also help you craft your message to potential suitors. A clearly defined and crisp message around what your business does, what problems it solves, and how it brings value to customers is an essential and powerful tool when marketing your business for sale. There is no better practice than making that case to your customers.

16.

Have I Implemented Good Systems to Produce Backlog Reports?

The buyer of your business can only receive a return on their investment through positive cash flows generated in the future. All buyers will want to get off to a good start as soon as possible after closing the transaction.

Therefore, it is imperative that you can produce an accurate backlog report of sold or in-process orders that will turn into future revenues and cash flows. Prospective buyers will want to see this information early in the due diligence process and periodically right up to closing of the transaction. Furthermore, if you are purchased by a public company, you will have to create a backlog report to be incorporated into their required disclosures.

Backlog is typically defined as sold orders for the future production and delivery of materials and the future provision of services. It is different than your sales funnel, which lists outstanding quotations and sales opportunities and may indicate a level of confidence that the order or project will be won. Conversely, backlog is future revenues already sold.

It is important to both properly define backlog specific to your company and to develop processes and reports to calculate an accurate backlog on a regular basis, such as monthly.

In addition to sold orders for materials not yet shipped or services not yet rendered, many backlog calculations include:

- The annual value of contracted recurring revenues,
- The annual value of non-contracted but highly predictable recurring revenues, and
- The remaining value under long-term contracts, such as construction contracts.

Backlogs vary significantly by industry, sales cycle, and, to a lesser degree, business model. Some industries, such as construction, have long and typically large backlogs in which revenues are highly predictable for the next 6 to 18 months or even longer. Other industries have short backlogs of 30 to 60 days before existing orders must be replaced with new ones.

Prospective buyers will be examining whether your backlog is consistent with expectations for your industry. If a commercial construction contractor's backlog indicates that only 25 percent of the next six months of forecasted revenues have been sold, a decline in revenues may be likely in the near future and new ownership might need to focus on not only bringing in a normal level of sales orders but also enough to replenish the backlog.

Likewise, if thirty-day backlogs are common in your industry, but your company's backlog consistently averages seventy days, then a prospective buyer should have a high degree of confidence that the company's revenues will remain strong during months immediately after closing the transaction.

The key is to have this information available, work on correcting weaknesses in the backlog if necessary, and be able to demonstrate to a prospective buyer the ebbs and flows of backlog levels through various business cycles and seasons.

17.

Is My Business Growing Consistently?

Not surprisingly, growing businesses are more attractive and earn higher valuations than flat or declining businesses. Again, the buyer of your business only achieves a return on their investment from the future cash flows of the business. Therefore, a consistently growing business is more likely to meet or even exceed the buyer's targeted rate of return on his investment than a stagnant business without a history of consistent growth. In a piece for InvestmentBank.com, Nate Nead of Deal Capital Partners, LLC put it this way:

> *"High-growth firms that can show a trend that does not appear to have the potential of abating anytime in the near future will almost always receive a higher multiple for valuation—all things being equal. The assumption is that if growth continues to march forward at a similar pace, the buyer will be able to capture the excess value. The tip to business owners is simply this: build momentum for an upswing in revenue and profitability and then sell into it."*

Growth is a sign of health and vitality in a business.

Growing businesses foster a culture where change is constant and normal.

Growing businesses consistently add new people, exposing themselves to the talent market in a dynamic way. These new employees bring new energy, new ideas, and new leadership into the company.

For potential buyers of a business, consistent growth of the target company means

- They can recoup their investment at a faster rate as time goes by,

- The target and its management are conditioned to a quicker pace of making decisions and taking risks, and

- The target is most likely keeping up with market growth and may be taking market share away from competitors.

We all know that the market does not always allow for growth. Sometimes maintaining revenue levels and holding at a steady market share is a win.

Also, as many business owners begin to think about their ownership transition, they may be reluctant to make big bets by investing capital and effort into opening new markets or establishing new product and service lines. That is understandable.

However, for those owners who are planning on a potential sale of the business two to four years in the future, we believe that modest investments of time and financial resources toward achieving growth rates at least equivalent to the market will be rewarded with higher valuations for the company.

18.

Is My Business Seasonal?

If you have a highly seasonal business, you know it. You know how the cash flow changes, when to hire your seasonal work force, and how much cash to sock away for the next season's rush.

Buyers, however, may perceive seasonality as a risk unless they are already deeply familiar with your industry. Investment funds and banks who help finance acquisitions also perceive seasonality as a risk.

There a several ways to mitigate or at least dampen this risk. In a piece for Forbes. com, management consultant George Bradt stated that Prophase Labs, the maker of Cold-EEZE®, has mitigated some of the inherent seasonality of a cold-season product with a three-pronged approach: "leveling out revenues, curtailing costs, and engaging in complementary efforts."

To level out revenues, Prophase uses off-season campaigns to remind customers that summer colds do happen, and they need to be prepared with Cold-EEZE® on hand.

Your business may be able to level out revenues as well. What else can you do with the equipment you already own? Alternatively, what do your customers need during your off-season? If your business is reliant on seasonal travel from tourists or business travelers, find out what the locals need after all the visitors have gone home.

Finally, find out the alternative ways people are using your product. Newell Brands, the parent of Elmer's Glue, enjoyed a growth surge in 2017 when social media sites exploded with recipes to make homemade slime with Elmer's. Commercial or industrial companies should talk to other industries and people who use your products to see what alternative applications they have developed.

To curtail costs, Prophase Labs manages its off-season costs by minimizing marketing costs. It does enough marketing to support its summer cold effort and maintain brand awareness, but its investment is significantly less. It also levels out its production by building inventory in the off-season, which limits peak season overtime costs and allows for a flexible work schedule for part of the year.

Other ways to smooth costs are to assign staff to implement new technologies or perform major facilities or equipment upgrades during down times. In the accounting profession, we use the weeks between busy seasons to train staff, execute Lean Six Sigma programs, hold off-site strategy sessions, and assist clients with their special projects. The keys are to create the most value possible from the fixed portion of your labor costs, then eliminate or reduce as much variable cost as possible.

In another example from Prophase Labs, an allergy relief medicine was launched in 2017. The new medicine is a complementary product that uses much the same manufacturing, operational, and organizational processes as the company's cold medicine but with opposite seasonality.

Examples of this approach abound. Landscapers plow snow in the winter. Coffee houses offer exotic iced coffee flavors in the summer. Colleges fill dorms with kids attending specialty camps between semesters.

In addition to any attempts to mitigate the impact of seasonality, you should carefully document the various processes you use to manage seasonality in your business. While you may be able to manage the multitude of issues by gut feeling as discussed in Question 12, a prospective buyer will find comfort if 1) the processes to manage cash, labor, and off-season initiatives are well documented, and 2) action items are dispersed across the organization and not totally reliant on your effort and experience.

Finally, understanding the impact of seasonality on your working capital could be crucial in a transaction, depending upon when the deal closes. If there is meaningful seasonality in the business, working capital should be documented monthly over several on- and off-seasons so you will understand the implications of closing a transaction at various points in the year.

Working capital adjustments can often amount to 5 percent or more of transaction value, so it will be worth your time to document the impact of seasonality on cash needs. In most cases, as the seller you will be arguing for as low a working capital target at closing as possible, which will enable you to push the value of the transaction higher. Without good historical data at your fingertips, you will be arguing against a buyer who will want as much cushion in the working capital as they can get.

19.

Do I Have a Process to Forecast My Future Operating Results?

The most valuable companies in any industry are earning above-average profits, are growing at least as fast as their market, and are demonstrating they can predict their results based on a set of reasonable assumptions about market conditions.

Unfortunately, many lower middle market and smaller companies do not attempt to forecast their future results.

You can rest assured that one of the first requests that potential buyers or your investment banker or broker will make is to see a forecast of the next two to three years' results. You will not put your best foot forward if your first attempt at a forecast is when you prepare for a sale or respond to an unsolicited buyer's request. In most cases, deal talks will not proceed to valuation without your providing this information.

Like every other principle discussed in this book, this exercise will make your business better today even if you do not plan to sell for many years.

When preparing a forecast in anticipation of a transaction, you will lean toward more optimistic assumptions to increase forecasted future cash flows. That is expected. But when preparing forecasts for planning resource allocations and capital investment decisions in the coming twelve to thirty-six months, the process itself is equal in importance to the result.

We highly recommend establishing an annual process in which you forecast your results for the next two to three years and revisit the forecast at least semi-annually to review and adjust.

Employing a diligent and thoughtful approach to this process will force you to:

- Identify the key drivers of revenues and profits in your business

- Thoughtfully analyze what decisions and investments it will take to grow your business

- Consider whether you have capacity to expand production or service delivery

- Investigate your business and challenge any activities that are not producing the desired results

- Methodically fill information gaps to make better decisions

- Calculate the implications of your planned growth on working capital and capital expenditures

- Identify and deal with excess capacity in your selling, general, and administrative cost structure

- Contemplate if your desired growth rate can be achieved through market growth or if you will need to take market share from competitors or even possibly buy a competitor.

Assumptions are the most important ingredient in a forecast. You will understand your business at an even deeper level by creating a regular habit of thinking through the key assumptions that drive results, then measuring your results against those assumptions.

A forecast provides a tangible target for your employees to shoot for. Quality people aspire to achieve big goals, and employing this exercise will give your team a clear understanding of what "winning" means to you.

Financial Condition and Capital Structure Questions to Ask Before You Sell Your Business

20.

Does My Balance Sheet Reflect the Assets Owned by Each Legal Entity?

It is likely your business is really several legal entities operating together to provide your goods and services. Legal advisors often recommend multiple legal entities to isolate liability risks and to achieve certain tax advantages.

Often overlooked, however, are the record-keeping rigors required to achieve those advantages. Over time, record-keeping and contracting may become sloppy, resulting in a mismatch between actual ownership of buildings, machinery, equipment, and rolling stock and the legal entity that has claimed those assets on its books.

Further complicating this issue, the ownership of the entities may be different. An entity designed to own the underlying real estate of a company may have a separate owner than the operating company. A third company, designed to serve certain high-risk markets, may be partly owned by its own leader, while you or your family own the majority stake in all three companies.

When a transaction is in process, these issues will come to the forefront. The buyer may prefer not to purchase land and buildings from the existing owners and elect to pay rent instead. However, the buyer will likely want ownership and title to IT assets, production equipment, and the vehicle fleet to operate the business. If the legal and accounting records are not in sync, transactions can be delayed and desired tax treatments can be lost.

Usually, these issues can be resolved by creating the proper legal documents to re-title assets to the desired entity. But if these entities have different ownership structures and minority owners with strong voting rights, negotiation and additional consideration may be needed to transfer assets in or out of these entities.

Finally, it is not just hard assets such as real estate and buildings that need to be maintained in their appropriate legal entities. Other important assets such as accounts receivable and inventories should also carefully be maintained by each entity. The buyer may want to only purchase your primary domestic operating entity. But if, for the sake of convenience, your accountant mixed customer receivables, inventories, and vendor payables associated with your high-risk entity with your primary operating entity, you will be striving to carve out these assets and their impact to present an accurate picture to the buyer. In addition, this practice probably obliterated the liability protections you were trying to achieve by creating distinct entities in the first place.

These issues are unlikely to kill a deal, but they often delay and complicate transactions, and every delay increases the risk that new issues will come to light that will kill the deal.

21.

Is There Significant Deferred Maintenance on My Facilities or Key Equipment?

In my more than thirty years of experience in accounting and finance, I have had only one business owner brag to me that he bought his manufacturing and fabrication company after only driving by the facility.

You will not be as lucky as the original owners of that facility turned out to be.

Most prospective buyers will tour your facility before even making an offer. They will use this initial visit to try to gauge the level of attention you pay to maintenance of the company's operating assets. Developing a strong culture of maintenance for both facilities and equipment will project a positive image of the company to a prospective buyer.

In transactions that progress to due diligence, buyers will inspect maintenance records on all key equipment and look for proof that the facilities' key systems, such as HVAC, for example, have been consistently maintained.

For capital-intensive businesses, buyers will perform a detailed inspection of the facility and its systems. Often these inspections will be performed by industrial engineers from the buyer's staff or by qualified industry consultants. The buyer may hire experts from the manufacturer to inspect highly specialized equipment and determine how well it has been maintained and its remaining useful life.

A few years ago, we were engaged by a client to perform financial due diligence on a large retail facility. Parallel to our work, the client's facility experts were evaluating the building's structural integrity and primary systems. Because initial findings were concerning, they hired outside structural and mechanical engineers to perform a more detailed investigation.

This transaction never closed. Despite positive results of the financial due diligence and a good strategic and cultural fit for our client, our client could not overcome the risks and potential additional capital investment related to the poor condition of the building and its systems.

For the seller, the damage was significant. In addition to the legal and accounting fees incurred, the owners had to restore trust with key employees who had been told about the potential transaction and who then had to cancel strategic decisions about their post-closing pursuits. They were forced to recommit themselves to the business and begin working to correct the structural and maintenance issues at their facility.

These issues could have been avoided with a long-term commitment to make smaller investments into maintaining company assets along the way.

It is not just traditional real estate and manufacturing equipment that will be highly scrutinized during the due diligence process. Every company is now run by mission-critical technology systems. Expect buyers to do a deep analysis on your IT security systems and the costs that may be needed to bring hardware and software up to their standards.

The best companies are committed to strong maintenance programs that protect their investments in their assets. These companies understand the cost of unplanned downtime and use preventative maintenance programs or even more advanced equipment monitoring and predictive maintenance programs to mitigate their risks. This level of commitment will add another layer of confidence in the minds of prospective buyers as they evaluate your business.

22.

Will Significant Investments Be Needed to Expand My Business Organically?

It is important to position your company with prospective buyers as a growing, thriving business that will sustain strong cash flows into the future. Depending on the economic cycle of the industry and the overall economic environment in your markets, additional investments in facilities, equipment, or staff may be required to accelerate growth. Again, it is vitally important to consider these issues at least two to three years ahead of a proposed transaction.

Investment bankers tell us that sellers often make the mistake of waiting too late to make key investments to generate growth. Investments such as plant expansions, purchases of new production equipment, workforce training, and implementation of new technology systems need time to mature.

When those investments are made well ahead of a transaction, the returns on those investments will be reflected in the financial statements in the form of higher EBITDA levels.

In some industries, the investment required to expand market share to the next level may be significant. For example, in an industry in the early stages of robotic automation, a business owner may not be able to recoup the investments required to transform equipment, staffing, and processes to meet his or her exit timeline. In such cases, it may be appropriate to accelerate a potential sale of the business before customer bases and related cash flows are eroded.

Again, timing and planning are critical to this evaluation. We have seen instances where sellers are so locked into their personal timetables for exiting their business that they fail to appreciate the impact that eroding market share and falling behind their competitors will have on their transaction value.

Even if you choose not to make the investments required to take your business to its next level of growth, having a thoughtful, written expansion plan will be of value to a prospective buyer.

We like to ask owners what it would take to expand their business by 20 to 25 percent. Too frequently, we get weak answers that clearly have not been thought through or tested with real modeling of the owner's assumptions.

A well-crafted investment plan may not close a transaction or increase your business's valuation, but do not forget that a substantial portion of the transaction value is likely to be paid to you after the closing and may very well be contingent upon future results. It is worth your effort and in your best interests to lend your experience to shaping your business's future and mitigating potential investment missteps by the new owner.

23.

Do I Have Strong Controls and Accurate Records of My Inventory?

Inventory management may well be the hardest thing in business. We observe few middle market and smaller organizations that ace this area of their businesses. They can invent, design, build, sell, and install their widgets, but they struggle to keep track of them and the raw materials it takes to make them.

Companies underestimate impact of poor inventory management on working capital, labor costs, customer satisfaction, and exposure to fraud. As a result, they underinvest in people, processes, and systems and default to a strategy we have named "managing inventory by having plenty." Since no company wants to run out of an inventory item and because the management system has proven unreliable, the organization, usually unconsciously, keeps plenty (i.e., too much) inventory on hand.

Poor inventory management inevitably results in an overinvestment in working capital, excess inventory that must be deeply discounted or discarded, obsolete inventory that has been replaced by newer models or different technology and wasted labor costs as personnel spend valuable time searching for misplaced or missing inventory.

Poor inventory controls are also a major source of fraud in companies of all sizes. Employees with knowledge of the inventory and the market can take advantage of the lack of oversight and controls to monetize the inventory for personal gain.

Some companies expose themselves to fraud and other risks because they do not even realize they are in the inventory management business. Not long ago, we were engaged by a client to investigate a potential fraud associated with the client's refurbished parts inventory. This company earned revenues by transporting people across the country and around the world under contracts with private and governmental organizations. However, it also maintained its fleet of aircraft, which required an extensive inventory of refurbished parts and cannibalized spare parts from decommissioned aircraft.

The process of sending parts out for refurbishment and updating the manual inventory system was overseen by one person who was underqualified for the role and virtually unsupervised. Consequently, a clever and unscrupulous refurbishment vendor duped the inventory manager into sending him parts that he then refurbished and sold on the open market for his own benefit. Since there was no system for tracking parts in and out the refurbishment cycle, the vendor was able to keep the scam going until the company ran out of high-demand parts they were certain should have been available for refurbishment.

For this company, the amount or even fact of the fraud was not the primary issue: that was the devastating impact the fraud had on their fleet operations. They had failed to recognize the importance and the associated operating risks of not having a set of strong internal controls and processes over the inventory of spare parts. In their minds, they were in the transportation business, not inventory management.

In addition to the ongoing advantages of lower investment in working capital, operational efficiencies, and reduced risk of fraud, a well-run inventory can position your company to earn a premium valuation from a prospective buyer. Conversely, major issues in the valuation of inventory and the processing of inventory transactions can quickly erode confidence in overall operations, and valuation of your business may decline.

24.

Is There Significant Obsolete Inventory on My Balance Sheet?

Unsalable or otherwise obsolete inventory on the balance sheets of lower middle market and middle market companies is so prevalent, we have come to expect it in our practice.

When we conduct site visits for due diligence assignments, the owner or warehouse manager will often guide us by rows and rows of full shelves of inventory while boasting they have whatever a customer might need on the shelf, ready to go. We typically translate those words to mean, "We have tons of stuff that is most likely never going to sell."

In a transaction, the buyer will not pay for inventory that does not have a high likelihood of selling. During the due diligence process, the buyer will ask for a report of obsolete inventory, which typically lists each inventory item and the date it was last sold, or, for raw materials and component items, when it was last used in production. In most industries, inventory items not sold or used in the last six months will be adjusted out of the balance sheet for determination of closing working capital. If obsolete inventory has been present for several years, the buyer will write off that inventory in the calculation of adjusted EBITDA in those periods.

Back and forth negotiations and arguments over the value of inventory can create significant friction in a transaction and cause both parties, but particularly the seller, to lose sight of the big picture, which is to foster confidence in the transaction process.

To avoid keeping obsolete inventory, manage your inventory regularly and decisively. Reviewing slow-moving inventory reports quarterly or, at minimum, annually will give you the opportunity to take action that could minimize losses later. These actions might include offering pricing discounts, bundling slower-moving items with faster-moving ones, requiring warehouse personnel to use older versions of parts before newer versions are ordered and used, or selling parts internationally to prevent impacting your own markets. Proactivity is essential. The list of options available for dealing with obsolete inventory almost always shrinks with time.

In our experience, it is better to regularly review your inventory for obsolescence and take aggressive action to liquidate that inventory and extract some value from it now than to hold, store, count, and move it while you hope for a once-in-a-blue-moon customer who desperately needs that particular piece of equipment and is willing to pay a premium for it. Even if that "unicorn" of a customer need does arise, it rarely justifies maintaining all those inventory items to make one sale.

When efforts to wring value out of the obsolete inventory have failed, scrap the inventory and move on. Surprisingly, the act of writing off inventory is highly emotional for most business owners. Understandably, it is an admission that either a poor decision was made or something did not go as planned. No one likes to admit mistakes, particularly when there is a tangible price to be paid. But like most tough business decisions, it is best to get this admission over with and transition your attention to issues that can create or preserve value for your company.

Many sellers who have not dealt with their obsolete inventory issues go into a transaction hoping the buyer will overlook the issue. That could happen, but more often a sophisticated buyer or one with professional assistance will investigate the salability of the inventory. Even if inventory is not a key aspect of the transaction, buyers will wonder what other issues in the business have also not been dealt with.

As an example, a client engaged us to conduct due diligence on a potential acquisition target before offering the target company a letter of intent to purchase the business. After looking at the balance sheet and relating it to the seller's business model, we believed the inventory on the balance sheet was likely overstated due to obsolete inventory, and we urged our client to walk through the warehouse and make his own observations and inquiries. He took our advice, and while the buyer was walking through the warehouse and asking some probing questions, the seller admitted that approximately 75 percent of the inventory on the balance sheet was essentially worthless. This issue, coupled with a few others, led our client to move on to look at other targets.

In cases like that one, the seller could have avoided the issue by dealing with obsolete inventory before prospective buyers reviewed overstated balance sheets and before they toured the warehouse.

A final word on this issue for a specific set of business owners. Some companies in the value-added reseller space as well as companies who manufacture, install, and maintain complete systems (applies across many industries) often have the opportunity to take in older systems as trade-ins or essentially haul away the old systems as a service to their customer. As a result, these businesses can cannibalize these older systems for parts to service their customer base who still operate those systems. Given the minimal cost of these service spare parts, their sale can generate substantial gross profit margins.

In our experience and across many industries, there are typically one to five parts on a trade-in system for which there is market value. The remaining components are essentially scrap because the market is saturated with them. Despite this reality, it is also our experience that instead of inventorying the five parts with market value and scrapping the remaining parts, companies inventory the entire used system, including the dozens of parts that will likely never sell.

Even though these used systems were acquired with minimal or even zero financial investment, there is still a cost to maintaining them in your inventory year after year. Most companies count their inventory one to four times per year, and I can assure you it is demoralizing for employees to count the same items year after year knowing that eventually this inventory will probably be scrapped or sent to the landfill. Furthermore, inventory takes up space that must be rented or purchased and often must be stored in a climate-controlled space to prevent damage to delicate electronic components, which in turn drives higher utility costs.

Dealing proactively and decisively with obsolete inventory will help you maintain a low cost structure throughout the time you own and operate your business. It will also eliminate one more discussion during the transaction process that could slow down or derail a deal.

25.

Are My Fixed Asset Records Accurate?

Many companies maintain poor records of their fixed assets. Assets that have been disposed of or replaced remain on the books, inflating the gross value (i.e., the value before accumulated depreciation) of all assets. In other cases, depreciable assets are not well labeled and are lumped together into giant groups of assets such as "Equipment Purchases—2019."

For capital-intensive businesses, prospective buyers will want to cross-reference some of the key operating assets from the accounting records with their physical presence in the manufacturing or warehouse facility. If the fixed asset records are cluttered with assets the seller no longer owns, this process will become tedious and confusing.

Additionally, the fixed asset records are a key source of information to the buyer for planning post-acquisition investment. Buyers will want to understand the age of key assets to assess their remaining useful lives and to plan for eventual replacement. This is especially true for technology-related assets. For example, if a buyer is contemplating the purchase of a professional services company with one hundred employees, all of whom have laptops, the buyer will want a record of each computer's age to plan for eventual replacements.

While unlikely to derail a deal, needing to reconstruct fixed asset records during due diligence will slow down the deal, invite additional questions, and call into question the accuracy and veracity of other information provided during the transaction process.

26.

Do I Bill My Customers Promptly?

Most transactions are structured on a cash-free, debt-free basis and require the seller to deliver a closing balance sheet to the buyer on the day of closing that contains a targeted level of working capital that has been negotiated by the parties.

In this scenario, the seller keeps all the cash in the bank at closing but must pay off all debt except any incurred in the normal course of the business, such as amounts owed to vendors and employees. Debt repayment usually comes from both cash on hand and a portion of the sale proceeds.

Additionally, the seller must leave enough working capital that business operations can continue without immediate additional capital infusion from the buyer.

These terms are representative of most deals, but every element of every deal is negotiable, fact and circumstance specific, and highly dependent on the definition of terms.

Deal negotiations and structuring are outside the scope of this book. However, a general understanding of the importance of working capital in most deals is critical to the discussion of billing customers promptly and accurately, as well to the subject of having formal collections processes (the subject of Question 27).

Besides inventory, as discussed in Questions 23 and 24, accounts receivable is usually one of the largest and most important elements of a company's working capital. It is also highly influenced by policy, procedure, and management.

Accounts receivable is essentially loaning money to customers to ease the sales process. In most industries, extending credit to customers for fifteen to sixty days is customary and ingrained in the way vendors and customers interact with each other in the normal course of business.

Extending credit to customers is a use of working capital, that is, a use of your company's cash, because it extends the time that cash is received from the date of sale to some date in the future. Therefore, the more time you give your customers to pay you, the more you will have to subsidize your own operations with cash from other sources, such as banks and vendors.

The size of investment in accounts receivable varies widely from industry to industry, and even within an industry, the cash tied up in accounts receivable varies from company to company. Because of that variance, policies, habits, and good management can make a significant difference.

Many companies fall into the habit of billing all their activities at the end of the month. This practice puts tremendous pressure on the organization to focus on billing for several days or even a week after the end of each month, instead of focusing on customers. Just as critical, this habit delays cash receipts on those revenues by five to thirty days.

We often observe these habits in project-based or ticket-based business models. It is a natural organizational tendency to focus on the demands of project schedules and reduce ticket queues until the last possible moment, focusing on paperwork and invoicing only when there is a looming deadline, usually the month-end accounting close. The result is a compressed time schedule, an increased likelihood of errors, and a stretching of the cash flow cycle.

Errors occur because data needed to bill the customer, such as hours worked or materials used, is not recorded in real time, while work is being performed, and must be reconstructed during the billing process. This habit is surprisingly prevalent in middle market service companies because there is such a high priority on fixing the customer's issue and moving on to the next problem that data collection falls to the wayside. This habit is also highly inefficient, as each service must be revisited to prepare the billing.

The best companies bill every day or no less often than every week. Doing so requires excellent management, accurate data collection about revenue events in near real-time, and a consistent invoicing process that does not sacrifice customer service or on-time shipments.

To illustrate the impact on working capital of improving these processes, let's assume your company's revenues are $1,000,000 per month. Currently, you bill each month's revenues approximately 5 days after the close of each month, and customers pay you on average in 30 days, which coincides with your standard pay terms. Under these assumptions, your company will need to borrow from the bank or from your cash to pay vendors and employees for 50 days to operate your business. This represents your "investment in accounts receivable." The 50 days is calculated as follows:

- 15 days (half of the month), the average number of days you are extending credit to your customers before you bill them
- 5 days in the billing process
- 30 days in the average collection period.

The dollar value of this investment is $1,643,836:

- Average sales per day is $32,876.71 ($12,000,000 ÷ 365)
- Average number of days extending credit to the customer is 50
- Total invested equals $32,876.71 × 50 days (i.e. $1,643,836)

The impact of adjusting your billing practices to bill every day on the day after the service is provided would be a reduction in investment in accounts receivable of 38 percent, or $624,658. This is $624,658 in cash no longer needed to support your business operations just by improving your processes and is calculated as follows:

- Total days invested in accounts receivable would drop to 31 as follows:

  - 0 days invested in extending credit to your customers before you bill them

  - 1 day in the billing process

  - 30 days in the average collection period

- The dollar value of this investment would be $1,019,178:

  - Average daily sales of $32,876.71 × 31 days = $1,019,178

The difference is $624,658 ($1,643,836 minus $1,019,178), or 38 percent less cash invested in your business to support your extension of credit to customers.

In a transaction the seller will likely be required to leave sufficient working capital in the business to support its current operations. If your current operations require 50 days to support accounts receivable, then the buyer will rightly negotiate hard for that level of investment to be provided in the company at closing. Using the figures from the example, this would result in nearly $625,000 in cash handed over to the buyer that he can eventually extract from your business with better billing practices.

Your business model will determine the billing practices you can employ. For example, project-based businesses do not lend themselves to daily or even weekly billing. Instead, milestone billings may be more appropriate or even mandated in customer contracts. However, even in those instances, we see companies poorly manage their billing processes and weeks or even months may elapse before milestones are examined and bills are processed. This lackadaisical approach can increase working capital needs by hundreds of thousands of dollars.

Conversely, your business model may lend itself to an opportunity to bill your customers before you perform services. If you have created a recurring revenue business model that allows for monthly fixed-fee billings to customers, you should structure contracts to allow billing at the beginning of the month for that month's service rather than at the end of the month to reduce your investment in working capital by up to thirty days. Many companies with recurring revenue models go a step further and require their customers to allow them to draft the monthly fee from their bank account at the beginning of each month. In this scenario, the customer is financing your business rather than the other way around. Since these approaches are becoming more and more prevalent, they should rarely create pushback from customers, particularly new customers.

Running your business efficiently, particularly in the management of your working capital, is good business, whether you are in the process of selling or not. It takes hard work to move the organization to this level of execution, but the rewards are significant. And it will mean additional cash in your pocket if your business transitions to new ownership.

27.

Have I Implemented Processes to Get My Invoices Paid On Time?

The importance of ensuring your customers pay on time should be clear given the discussion and illustration in Question 26 regarding your billing practices. Additionally, one of biggest elements to the negotiated target level of working capital is accounts receivable, that is, the amount of money your customers owe you at any given time.

In general, the definition of accounts receivable used to calculate targeted working capital excludes invoices more than ninety days old. Therefore, a key part of minimizing your investment in accounts receivable is to ensure timely collection of all invoices.

Good processes for collecting overdue invoices can nearly eliminate losses from bad debts. Furthermore, a pristine listing of accounts receivable with only a few well-understood problem accounts will greatly increase a potential buyer's confidence.

In our experience, most customers intend to pay their invoices and pay them on time. Often, the issues that delay prompt payment are related to the company's internal processes or to poor execution of the sales or service transaction. Beyond those issues are those customers who habitually pay vendors late or who are experiencing financial strain.

The key is to discover the cause of payment delays as early as possible and address their root cause. Reach out to customers consistently, just before or just after the due date of their payment. Too many companies wait until invoices are already sixty or ninety days old before they attempt to find out what issues are delaying payment. As a result, actions that could have been taken earlier are delayed, and sometimes the opportunity to correct them is lost altogether.

Because of the importance of this process on the company's cash flows and investment in working capital, we recommend executive leadership be involved. In the most effective collection processes we have observed, an executive of the company is present on a weekly call or at a weekly meeting to review past-due accounts and ensure issues are being identified and corrected. Executive management's involvement will prevent collections tasks from being squeezed out by more urgent but less impactful issues. We are aware of one CEO of a billion-dollar organization who is actively engaged in weekly collection update meetings. If he believes collections activities are that important to his business, it is probably that important to yours as well.

Consider a few other effective collection procedures and practices we have seen:

- Hire personnel dedicated to the collection process or establish clarity that collections work as an essential responsibility of certain employees. In most middle market and lower middle market organizations, it may not be feasible to have personnel solely dedicated to collections. It is possible, however, to clarify that collections are an essential part of some employees' job responsibilities, not something to be done only when they have available time or when the company is experiencing a cash shortage.

- Sales personnel can be a resource in the collections process, but do not make them responsible for collections. Because salespeople are usually focused on pleasing the customer—and asking customers to pay is usually not an ingredient for making them happy—most salespeople are ineffective at collections. Nevertheless, the salesperson often has critical information about transactions that can help resolve payment delays.

- Likewise, do not allow sales personnel to control the customer account such that the collections staff cannot do their jobs effectively. Too often, a customer will respond negatively to a collection call, and the salesperson will demand that "no one is allowed to call this customer but me," or "you have to tell me anytime you are going to talk to my customer." Such rules are unworkable and ineffective, and management should not allow them to continue. If a customer is so prickly about paying their invoices on time, there are deeper issues in this business relationship that executive management should explore.

- Focus intermittently on the twenty-five largest past-due invoices or customer accounts. Many times, particularly when cleaning up receivables that have been neglected and allowed to age for months beyond their due date, it is good to break up the accounts receivable aging report to focus collection efforts on making the biggest dollar impact possible rather than just working the list as it prints from your accounting system.

Implementing an effective and consistent process for collecting accounts receivable will reduce your investment in working capital, make your company more attractive to potential buyers, and help drive potential buyers' confidence about the quality of your business.

28.

Do I Have an Effective Purchase Order and Accounts Payable Process?

Prospective buyers will have a vested interest in the processes and controls over your procurement and accounts payable systems.

These areas are the ripest for fraud in middle market and lower middle market companies. Because staff in small companies often serve in several capacities, too much control is often concentrated in a few individuals. Often, there is a bookkeeper, controller, or purchasing agent who has achieved a high degree of trust with the owner and has the ability to manipulate processes to hide fraud. Also, companies tend to outgrow the systems and processes that were effective when the business was small, leaving them wide open for exploitation when the business grows.

Implementing a sound purchase order and accounts payable system can alleviate most of these risks. By requiring documentation and approval of purchases made on the company's behalf, followed by a segregated system of vendor invoice matching, approval, and disbursement processing, even smaller companies with limited staff can achieve proper segregation of duties.

Prospective buyers examining the controls over these functions at your company want to be assured that 1) there is not an ongoing fraud occurring in the business, and 2) their controls and procedures over purchasing and disbursements will be culturally acceptable to employees.

Procedures and controls always need to be attuned to the size and complexity of the business. There is no point in overburdening employees or creating bureaucracy to prevent all imaginable fraud, but having a strong set of controls appropriate for your business will be valuable in a transaction.

Finally, it is not uncommon in our practice to see middle market and sometimes even smaller companies purchased by much larger, publicly held companies that are subject to Sarbanes-Oxley internal control reporting requirements. These companies are often willing to pay a premium over other buyers to achieve their strategic goals, and having an appropriate control environment over purchasing and disbursement functions will enable such buyers to more readily close a transaction with your company.

29.

Does My Line of Credit Revolve?

We have addressed important working capital issues in Questions 23, 24, 26, and 27. Prospective buyers can gauge your effectiveness in managing working capital by charting out the monthly balance of your revolving line of credit over the course of several years to understand the working capital requirements and determine whether the revolver reflects actual working capital fluctuations or points to other capital demanding issues.

The purpose of a revolving line of credit (often referred to its shorthand name "revolver") is to fund shortages in working capital during periods of rapid growth or seasonal shifts in the business. As your banker has probably sternly warned you, a revolver is not intended to fund losses in operations.

When a business experiences a growth spurt, it needs additional cash to fund purchases of raw materials, build up work in process inventory (which includes additional production labor costs), and finished goods. Growing businesses will also experience an increase in accounts receivable because of higher sales volumes.

Some of these cash needs can be financed by vendors, at least for a short period of time, as your accounts payable balances will also grow. But if your products and services require significant labor, your employees cannot be a source of short-term borrowing. They, of course, will need to be paid in the normal weekly or biweekly rhythm.

Many owners experience cash flow shortages in their business and do not understand why. The fastest way to find where your cash is going is to examine the cash flow statement.

The cash flow statement, often called the third financial statement after the balance sheet and income statements, provides insight into how cash is being used in your company. Generally, the statement begins with your net income, adjusts the net income for non-cash expenses such as depreciation, then shows how changes in the various elements of working capital (e.g., accounts receivable, inventory, and accounts payable) are affecting cash balances. The sum of these changes reflects the cash being earned or used in your business's operations. From there, the statement indicates the cash being used to purchase new equipment and cash being distributed to you, the owner. Finally, the statement will indicate cash you have received from new borrowings and that you have used to pay down previous borrowings.

Taking the time to understand the cash flow statement can transform your understanding of the financial workings of your business. The above summary of the statement is greatly simplified, and a deeper dive is outside the scope of this book, but if your controller, financial advisor, or CPA does not provide a cash flow statement each month, I encourage you to ask for one and for a lesson in how to read it.

As your business grows or experiences a seasonal surge in revenues, demands on your cash will typically grow, and a well-designed revolver is usually the appropriate solution to fund this need. In most cases it is well collateralized (secured by accounts receivable and inventory) and is set up as a short-term commitment. For example, the revolver is typically in place for one year with an expectation of annual renewal. As a result, it is one of the least expensive forms of capital you can use to support your business.

The concept is that as revenues level out from their growth spurt, you will collect outstanding receivables and pay down the borrowings on the revolver. The term "revolver" is derived from this expectation. The agreement or contract documenting the revolving line of credit with your bank may require that the balance of the revolver must reach zero for at least one day during the year. Banks sometimes require this of borrowers to keep them focused on the true need for this type of capital.

What does it mean if the revolver is not revolving—if the balance never reaches zero during the year? There are several possibilities, some good, but some could be of concern to a prospective buyer:

- Growth. If, instead of a burst of growth, the company is experiencing a prolonged, multiyear season of growth, then the revolver will likely not be paid down to zero during this time and may, in fact, need to be expanded to support the continued growth.

- Poor management of working capital. In most business models, demands on working capital follow patterns in revenue levels. In a manufacturing environment, working capital increases well in advance of revenues as the company buys raw materials, manufactures finished products, ships, and (sometimes) installs the products. These companies generally experience increases in their inventory balances followed by increases in accounts receivable before eventual receipt of payment from customers.

  Service companies, on the other hand, typically experience increases in accounts receivable as services are delivered and billed to customers. In either case, as well as in the myriad other business models prevalent in our economy, these business cycles put pressure on cash flows that can be supported by borrowings on the revolving line of credit. However, mismanagement of inventory and accounts receivable levels will exaggerate the pressure on cash flows and drive higher borrowings on the revolver. Furthermore, the revolver will not revolve (be paid down) in the expected pattern. These trends will be troublesome to a prospective buyer and will likely create additional inquiries and due diligence to understand the underlying issues.

- Distributions or dividends. A growing business requires capital, and company ownership should expect to have to reinvest some if not all of their profits into the growth of the company. However, owners who take cash out of the company in the form of distributions or dividends equal to or even exceeding company profits strain the company's working capital, and the revolver might not revolve predictably. Similar to the working capital management issues discussed above, buyers will want to understand these issues so they can project their working capital and borrowing needs under their ownership.

- Losses. By far the worst reason why a revolver is not revolving is that it is funding losses. Although every business experiences bad months, bad quarters, or sometimes even bad years, a consistent pattern of weak profitability or losses or will usually result in ever-increasing balances on the revolver and may stretch the company up to or past its borrowing limits. A revolver balance that is almost always at its limit is often a sign of underlying problems.

Whether or not your revolving line of credit is revolving will not kill a deal, but it could enhance or damage your position in negotiations over target working capital, as well as foster or erode the prospective buyer's confidence in your business.

30.

Is My Company's Debt Reasonable for My Business Model and Current Growth Rates?

In addition to reviewing the activity in the revolving line of credit, we recommend owners think through their overall debt levels well in advance of any potential transaction. Debt is a useful and relatively inexpensive tool to fund growth. Used wisely in a well-managed business, debt can help accelerate growth rates and expansion into new markets and new product lines.

However, because debt must be repaid, it can also put stress on a business by reducing the margin for error. In businesses carrying a high level of debt in relation to their shareholder equity and ability to generate profits (i.e. a highly leveraged business model), sometimes even a modest dip in revenues in just one quarter can create a significant strain on cash flows and management and can damage banking relationships.

When a revenue hiccup occurs in a highly leveraged business that has little cash to cushion the impact, the owner has less time and fewer resources to react. This pressure can force decisions that may have medium- to long-term consequences for the business, such as the loss of key personnel, premature shutdown of branch offices, elimination of product or service lines before they have had a chance to mature, or benefits cuts that depress staff morale.

These outcomes are better avoided in the one to four years before an attempted sale of the business. While you cannot typically control market events that create a blip in your revenues, you can structure your balance sheet and debt profile to make your company more resilient to such events.

Prospective buyers will assess the overall level of debt your business is carrying, and if it is relatively high, additional due diligence will be required to understand the underlying causes.

Profitable businesses with lower debt levels will always be more attractive to potential buyers than businesses operating under the pressures of heavy debt loads.

Strategic, Organizational, and Human Resource Questions to Ask Before You Sell Your Business

31.

Do I Have an Effective and Well-Functioning Management Team?

A talented management team is a value driver for your company.

Many buyers, particularly financial buyers, do not want to step into day-to-day management of the target company. Mergers and acquisitions advisor Steven Pappas of Touchstone Advisors stated in a 2018 article on "The Strategic Buyer vs. Financial Buyer: How Do They Differ?" that "the one thing financial buyers have in common is they typically invest in solid companies with strong management teams. They do not want to come in and manage the company. They want to invest capital, bring some synergies or strategic benefits, grow through additional acquisitions, and eventually sell a much larger company for a much higher multiple."

The value of attracting, training, and retaining good talent at key positions could not be stated any more clearly.

Many buyers' initial screening process requires the target company to demonstrate that their management team is effective in its roles. Some buyers will immediately discount companies that do not invest in talent for key positions such as president and sales, operations, and finance heads.

The other, potentially more important value-driving aspect of investing in talented professionals at key positions is the impact talent can have on the growth and scalability of the business. A strong management team will allow your company to grow faster and larger than could ever be possible with just you making all the decisions or with weak players who are unable to manage their key functions effectively through periods of rapid growth.

Bigger companies generally earn higher valuations than smaller companies. Growing companies generally earn higher valuations and are more salable than stagnant ones. One of the key ingredients to achieving these higher valuations is to have a talented management team in place several years in advance of a transaction to give the team time to demonstrate its abilities and become a cohesive integrated operating unit.

Business owners who fail to plan and invest ahead of a desired sale date will be faced with two choices: a more limited market for their company or a post-closing commitment to day-to-day leadership until new management is in place.

32.

Do All My Employees Know Their Roles and Responsibilities?

Most likely, your company will be purchased by either a larger organization in your industry or a financial buyer looking to grow your existing business quickly and combine it with additional businesses to create a much larger organization in a short time, usually two to five years. In either instance, your company will be more easily integrated and therefore more valuable as an acquisition target if everyone in your organization knows their roles and responsibilities.

In many organizations, lines of authority and accountability are weak. The result is that a few usually large and consequential customer orders go somehow awry. When this happens, a few talented individuals drop all their current work, jump in, and through heroic effort pull the project out of the fire. Organizations often become so conditioned to this routine, it becomes their standard operating procedure. Projects go sideways, the company calls in the heroes, and the organization runs from one operational crisis to the next.

Setting aside the negative impacts of these habits on profit margins and morale, if this scenario is common in your company, integrating your operations successfully into a larger organization or trying to quickly scale your operations will be painful and may lead to discounts in valuation or some buyers moving on to other targets who are more future ready.

Granted, the process of creating an appropriate and scalable organizational design coupled with good job descriptions and written processes is time consuming and tedious. But failing to address these issues will prevent your company from growing profitably and retaining great people. Employees do not like to come to work each day and get waylaid by the fire drill du jour. They will leave, and they will tell others that your organization is a hot mess. Conversely, employees thrive when their employer provides clarity about their roles and responsibilities and their routes to personal success.

33.

Do I Invest in Developing Employees to Their Full Potential?

In today's economy every company is a knowledge-based business. Service companies' primary assets are their people and the value they create for customers. But even for manufacturing companies that have invested heavily in automation, the knowledge and experience of the people running their sophisticated equipment is enormously valuable and must be nurtured.

Becoming a meaningfully people-focused organization is a great way to differentiate your business from other potential acquisition targets.

To foster a people-focused culture, companies should invest in programs that incentivize setting annual goals for personal development and for helping the company move forward. These programs might include earning increasingly higher certification levels on software or other systems the business uses. Nearly all mid-market and market-leading software manufacturers have multiple levels of user and administrator certification programs. Supporting employees' efforts to earn these certificates can significantly increase both the employees' value and their loyalty to your company. The same is true for manufacturing equipment and other systems.

Goal-setting should also include initiatives that directly create value for the company, such as removing time-wasting steps from processes, innovating ways to reduce errors, and taking the time to fix long-standing issues. A consistent and effective employee engagement process will facilitate this process and move individual performance to higher levels.

We recommend a "feedforward" approach endorsed by neuroscientist Dr. Robert Cooper of Cooper Strategic. According to Dr. Cooper, brain research indicates that giving employees positive attention (i.e., "feedforward") is thirty times more effective than the negative attention associated with providing feedback, which is typically viewed as a "flaw-finding" exercise. In a feedforward discussion, Dr. Cooper suggests statements such as "Building on everything we have learned, including what has not worked well, how can we be our best ever for what is next?"

Another often undervalued factor in employee development is continuous training and learning. One of the most value-driving practices a company can implement in its operations is narrowly targeted short-duration training sessions to help employees do one or two things more efficiently or more accurately.

For example, experienced machine operators could show others a few tips and tricks they have learned over the years that make their jobs easier. Office workers using common tools such as Microsoft Office can also benefit from such sessions. Many of us have watched someone work in Excel and suddenly asked, "How did you do that?" This kind of training can be accomplished in a quick fifteen-minute meeting on the shop floor or a thirty-minute lunch-and-learn session. Whatever the format, creating an environment where people are learning and helping each other improve enhances the value and culture of your workforce.

Finally, in some disciplines, the employee's stature in the market is significantly enhanced by obtaining more formal credentials. In our firm, the Certified Public Accountant designation is the gold standard for most of our work. However, we have certain niche practices such as business valuations and fraud investigations where other credentials carry weight with the market, and we encourage, support, and celebrate those achievements.

Inevitably, some employees will take advantage of your investments in their personal development and then accept job offers from your competitors or move to another industry entirely, taking their newly acquired skills and knowledge with them. If a preponderance of your best people take this route, there are likely other issues you need to address in your company's culture.

Employee development is one of the key ingredients in corporate culture, and culture is what makes or breaks most transactions for the buyer. Fostering a culture focused on employee development will make your company more attractive to potential buyers and will benefit you immeasurably in the meantime.

34.

Do I Have a Good Record of Employee Relations?

All buyers will investigate your history of employee relations and review all your employee files, including separated employees. If a buyer uncovers a pattern of harassment allegations, payment of settlements, or an indication that your company tolerates bad behavior, the transaction will be at risk.

No matter how strategic the transaction is for their business, no buyer will be willing to buy into a toxic employee relations culture with the hope of fixing it. Changing such a culture is too hard and too expensive in management time and real dollars.

Too many businesses tolerate bad behavior from certain individuals because of their perceived value to the organization. They are the best salesperson or the best technician, or they work magic with vendors on pricing and delivery schedules. In the meantime, they abuse or harass employees, cause great people to leave your organization, and create huge potential financial risks for your organization when an employee decides to take legal action against your company. You may have rationalized their behavior in the past, but it will catch up to you at some point, and it will be expensive when it does.

If you operate in a relatively small market, either geographically or with niche products and services, your employee relations reputation is likely well known by your competitors, suppliers, and prospective workforce. If your reputation in this area is poor, most buyers will never consider a transaction with you. It is simply not worth the risk or the effort.

If this area of your business needs to be fixed, start now.

35.

Do I Routinely Weed Out Low-Performing Employees?

"What took you so long?"

That was the question one of my key employees asked me one afternoon after I had terminated a longtime employee earlier in the day. The question stung because they were right. I had made some effort to work with this employee to improve their performance and adhere to our culture, but mostly I had ignored the issue and let my better performers pick up the slack. They quietly resented me for it. After the termination, department morale picked up immediately.

As you contemplate the possibility of a future transaction, workforce morale needs to be as strong as possible. In addition to investing in your employees' personal development and promptly dealing with bad behavior, you should also foster the habit of consistently weeding out the 5 to 10 percent of your workforce that does not perform at an acceptable level or practice the company's values on a day-to-day basis.

You can send no stronger positive message to your stars—the top 5 to 10 percent of your workforce—than to cull those employees who consistently make errors, who fail to jump in and help when additional effort is needed, and who complain that they are not getting raises and promotions despite their mediocrity.

Am I suggesting a cutthroat "one mistake and you are out" culture? Of course not. You should create a strong employee orientation program, provide clear job responsibilities, be a good coach, give multiple second chances, and provide ample time to improve performance.

But you should also be decisive. Leaders almost always know who their weak performers are. Usually, it is a matter of courage to make the decision and then have a compassionate and respectful conversation with the employee to facilitate their exit from the business. Your employees are counting on you to make these decisions and not let poor performance fester into a morale problem.

No buyer wants to acquire a weak workforce that desperately needs pruning. Both financial and strategic buyers know that acquirers are known for coming in and making drastic cuts in the target's workforce to cut costs.

The reality is that buyers are focused on growth. They strongly prefer to acquire a high-performing workforce they can use to quickly grow revenues and cash flows. While some pre- and post-transaction terminations are about eliminating redundant positions or cutting costs, most buyers are focused on the future and on executing their strategic objectives with their newly acquired assets and operations. They must have a great workforce to accomplish those goals. Taking time to identify and remove weak performers is time-consuming and expensive—it is not a task they want to do.

If your workforce has been continually pruned, refreshed, and positioned for growth, you will set your company apart from your competitors as a more valuable organization.

36.

Can My Business's Culture Be Successfully Merged Into Another Company?

Can you imagine a major airline such as American, United, or Delta successfully merging with Southwest Airlines?

Southwest is known for its unique people and operating culture. Flight attendants often deliver the required pre-flight safety announcements in song or with humorous tweaks. The airline is known for consistently on-time arrivals coupled with peanuts and a points-based (rather than miles-based) rewards system. Pilots and maintenance technicians must know only one airplane—the Boeing 737—reducing training costs and streamlining required maintenance programs.

In short, some of the key ingredients to Southwest's success and profitability are based in its unique culture. Conversely, this unique culture also makes it difficult for Southwest to grow via acquisition or be considered a target for acquisition.

Growth by acquisition, either by companies looking to acquire competitors or by investment companies seeking strong returns, is a high-risk strategy. Robert Sher, founding principal of CEO to CEO, an advisory company working with mid-market companies to navigate change, stated in a piece for Forbes that research indicates that success rates of mergers and acquisitions (meaning the transaction delivered the expected returns to the acquiror) is approximately 50 percent. I have seen research citing the success rate as low as 30 percent. Sher cites cultural fit as one of the top five reasons why acquisitions fail.

Hopefully, culture is a key aspect of your company's success. Healthy, sustainable cultures are attractive to potential buyers. However, some cultures, even at healthy companies, are so unique that the business is virtually unsalable. It is important to have a deep understanding of your own culture so that you can assess how well it might fit with other business cultures when potential buyers come knocking.

Given the stakes, it is a waste of time to go deep into a potential transaction without an honest, upfront assessment of the cultural fit between the two companies. Often, in middle market and smaller transactions, significant portions of the purchase price are paid after closing and may be dependent on the post-closing success of the merged companies. Forcing a transaction where you know the companies will struggle to come together culturally could be very expensive in the long run.

While transaction structuring is outside the scope of this text, for purposes of illustrating the risk associated with transaction proceeds being paid after the closing date, examples of post-closing payments include

- Seller loans or seller notes. In this arrangement, the buyer typically pays a portion of the purchase price in cash at closing and then signs a loan agreement to pay the seller the remainder of the purchase price over time, usually at a market rate of interest. These loan payments may or may not be contingent upon the level of success of the company in the months and years after the closing.

- Holdbacks. Holdbacks are typically used when there are unresolved issues as of the closing date. In these arrangements, a portion of the purchase price is put into an escrow held by a third party (typically a financial institution) until a certain event has occurred. Such events could include the resolution of a pending lawsuit, the lapse of a warranty period, the expiration of the statute of limitations on a potential claim, or the general passage of time to allow the risk of potential claims by third parties to diminish.

- Earn-outs. In these arrangements, a portion of the purchase price is paid after closing based on the achievement of certain milestones. Such milestones could include achieving a specified level of revenue growth or a defined amount of earnings in the period(s) after closing. Earn-outs are frequently used in transactions when the seller's valuation of the company is much higher than the buyer's view of valuation. The earn-out mechanism is used to "bridge the gap" between the two valuations such that if in fact, the acquired company delivers the level of profits and cash flows promised by the seller, then additional proceeds are "earned" and the buyer pays additional purchase price based on the earn-out formula in the transaction documents.

A transaction may include one, two, or all three of the above tools to accomplish its objectives. While the earn-out mechanism is almost always tied to the future success of the acquired company, payments under seller notes as well as holdbacks are also often tied to future performance.

Given these realities, it is essential that your company's culture can be successfully merged into another company. If not, you may risk never receiving a significant portion of the sales price. If you have built a successful company with a unique, one-of-a-kind culture, there are alternatives to monetizing the value you have created, including an employee stock ownership plan, selling the business to management, or passing it on to children.

All these options take considerable time for planning and successful execution, but they can deliver enormous value to you as you exit the business. It is important that you conduct a candid assessment of your company's culture, and if you conclude it will very difficult to fit it into another organization, you should start working on these alternatives far in advance of your desired exit from day-to-day responsibilities.

37.

Can All Key Day-to-Day Processes Run Without My Direct Involvement?

The less your business needs you each day, the more valuable it is to a prospective buyer.

When you have successfully addressed the previous six questions, you will have achieved the goal of separating yourself from the day-to-day operations of your business. You will need a strong management team, clear roles for all employees, a healthy culture, and high bar for employee performance. Once those pieces are in place, your company will be well positioned for new ownership to take it to even greater heights.

Strategic owners require their employees to practice running the company without them. They take extended time off and set clear expectations for management to make decisions and keep the company moving forward. In the process, management will make mistakes and must live with the consequences.

We once had a client that practiced this several times a year. He would purposely take extended vacations of two to three weeks and would not be readily available for phone calls or emails. During these periods, executive management carried on day-to-day operations of the company. They pushed projects to conclusion, they responded to customer issues, they resolved internal matters, approved and paid vendor bills, invoiced and collected payments from customers, and they proposed on new work. The owner made himself available in the event of a true emergency, but generally stayed out of day-to-day issues during these times.

Subsequently, when his company sold, the buyer placed significant value on the quality and experience of the management team and its ability to execute the company's day-to-day operations. At the closing, our client received ninety percent of the total purchase price and essentially walked away from the business.

Some owners take this a step further and do longer-term sabbaticals for 60 to 180 days. In these scenarios, management is forced to make even more difficult decisions that simply cannot be deferred until the owner returns. Such decisions include hiring and firing personnel, acquiring new equipment, investing in new markets, or adding new products or services. These periods build confidence in the management team and allow it to test its skills in making even more consequential decisions.

New owners want to grow your business rapidly. If your business is already positioned to operate at a high level and is not dependent on you for day-to-day decisions, it will be highly and positively differentiated from most other companies prospective buyers will consider. Your business's ability to function without you is an important driver of its value and salability.

38.

Is There Clarity About What My Business Does and Does Not Do?

The best companies do not chase revenues outside their wheelhouse. Their owners have considered and remember at all times what their companies specialize in, what they do and what they do not do.

Weaker companies cannot seem to resist the temptation to dabble in tangential markets, adjacent geographies, and supposedly easy, quick profits. They try to serve both large and small customers. They try to serve customers who are primarily focused on value, as well as customers who are primarily focused on price, often missing the mark on both.

The result is often stretched resources, damaged customer relationships, and depressed morale from employees straining to produce work that meets an unmanageable variety of expectations.

We work with a company that has struggled with this issue. Its primary business is to modify wireless towers when the mobile phone carriers roll out new technologies, such as 5G. The company is an expert in the antennas, radios, and switching gear that makes these technologies work.

Because of its relationships in the industry, our client became aware of and pursued a contract to provide fiber optic cable in-ground and on poles across many miles of various terrain. The project was in a state three states away from the company's primary geographical market.

They were lured into the contract by its huge size and the potential to win additional orders for more miles across this state. The hope was for a three- to five-year run executing this supposedly lucrative work.

The contract turned into a disaster as the ultimate customer, the state's government, was sued by existing telecommunications companies who were going to be displaced by the new technology. The litigation slowed the work and made funding uncertain.

Furthermore, the company had to rely on subcontractors who had the expertise and equipment to perform the work. Because the work dribbled out slowly due to the ongoing litigation, there was no way to make it efficient. These losses were exacerbated by the fact that the project was much more difficult than expected: because the company had been so enthralled with winning the contract, it failed to carefully scope the work and understand the potential problems. The company also failed to protect itself in contracts with subcontractors, so when problems arose, it paid extra fees to the subcontractors but were stuck with fixed fees with the customer. The result was the loss of hundreds of thousands of dollars and a tremendous distraction for management.

This company does not make these mistakes when working in its own area of expertise and geographic footprint. These were unforced errors that companies make when they fail to say "no" to opportunities that do not fit their business model.

Conversely, another client company, a plumbing subcontractor, is very disciplined in its approach. It focuses solely on projects with a high density of plumbing (i.e., many bathtubs, sinks, and toilets) in a repeatable application, such as military housing, university housing, and high-density multifamily apartment complexes. The company has built processes, procedures, and a customized smartphone application around these types of projects to control costs and quality.

Because of its discipline, this company has been able to expand its business into new geographic markets, though only when it can secure projects that fit its target customer set.

Does this company see opportunities to secure contracts on other construction applications? Yes. Every week. But it has defined what it does and does not do and sticks with it.

As a result, this company's value proposition to a potential buyer is clear. The company has built itself to function as a platform company, to roll up other competitors and achieve superior returns, by virtue of its adherence to a clear set of operating principles and the courage to say "no" to opportunities that do not fit its specialization.

When your business strays outside of what it does best, particularly in a one-off, opportunistic fashion, you face costs and risks that many business owners do not appreciate. Contracting with different customers and vendors may drive up legal costs and may require assumption of liabilities not normally assumed in your primary business. Project management is stretched thin due to unfamiliar processes. The contract may require investments in unfamiliar inventory or tools, additional training and technical certifications, or licensing with state or local governments. More and more often, large customers require a physical presence to be established in the work area, near the customer, or both, which may require expensive leasing of space. On top of all these items are all the issues that would fit under the umbrella of "unknown unknowns."

In our experience, pursuing these opportunities, or "chasing revenues" as we describe it, is not a good long-term strategy. There are no easy profits in business.

If you get lucky and can execute well on a particular project out of your wheelhouse, it will be money in your pocket, but it will probably not drive value into a sale transaction if it cannot be regularly duplicated. Conversely, if you show a regular pattern of chasing revenues that turn out poorly, you will strain to successfully argue those losses should be overlooked in the valuation of cash flows of the business.

39.

Do I View Information Technology as a Strategic Resource?

To be competitive in the future, every company must digitize or become irrelevant. For some businesses and industries, the future is already here.

We are quickly moving from an environment where technology is not just a requirement to improve employee productivity and quality of life but an essential part of the customer experience. Tirrell Payton, a San Diego–based technology consultant writing for business.com, states,

> *"These days, most of the leading-edge methods and practices being adopted in enterprise technology come from the consumer world. Whether it be mobile, social, or advances in design and interaction, there is a lot more crossover between consumer technology and business technology. This may seem irrelevant; but remember that your strategic partners, your customers, and even your employees operate in the consumer world as well. Therefore, customers expect their services and experiences to be customized and personal. This creates huge opportunity to create value by meeting*

their needs, but it will require an updated, more flexible execution model. Technology systems will need to be more lean and flexible to fully take advantage of new opportunities."

To summarize, value is created and preserved by moving your business to a more lean, flexible, digital model.

Digital businesses are easier to vet in due diligence and easier to integrate. Most importantly, they are great platforms for growth, as they allow you to add additional businesses that have not yet made the transition themselves. Buyers can at times acquire businesses at a discount because they have not invested in technology, then integrate them quickly into a digitized business model, accelerating the buyer's return on investment.

Below are five ideas to consider in transforming your approach to information technology (IT) from a cost of doing business into a competitive weapon with inherently more value to prospective buyers:

- Improve the customer experience. Creating a more elegant and engaging customer experience is the number one way to use technology to create a competitive advantage and make your company more valuable. The most impactful IT-driven companies are those whose technology is focused on the customer. How could your customers have an unexpected and unbelievable experience interacting with your company? What information do they need? How much faster and more elegantly could you provide it to them? Focusing IT innovation on the customer will generate powerful ideas that could disrupt your entire industry and change the trajectory of your company.

- Improve your employees' experience. Technology can be a huge morale booster. While it may be true that no one really likes change, it is a certainty that employees do not like manual and menial tasks that could be done by computers and algorithms. Concurrently investing in technology and training to help employees do higher-value work will let employees know that they are making a larger contribution to the success of your company.

- Improve the quality and efficiency of internal processes. Increasing the use of technology, particularly at the transaction and customer experience levels, will drive better and more efficient processes into your businesses. Too many companies must process entire transactions, or portions of every transaction, with some type of manual intervention. Sometimes this is the result of offering too many options to customers or making promises outside of policy. Well-designed technology systems typically have efficient embedded processes that drive down processing time, costs, and errors. Committing your company to using technology across all transactions will make it more nimble and competitive.

- Improve the speed and accuracy of data used to operate the business. When you use technology from start to finish in your transaction systems—from prospect management to collecting cash, paying vendors, and reporting results—you will be able to gather more information about your business faster and more accurately. Each manual step in the transaction or reporting stream slows down the overall process, increases the risk of error, and likely reduces the amount of data available in the system to report or analyze. A fully digitized quote-to-cash system will set your business apart from many others prospective buyers will review.

- Improve your brand in the market. Once you have used technology to create an awesome customer experience and improve the quality of life for your employees, you can leverage your successes to reposition your brand as a market innovator and leader. Customers, investors, vendors, and prospective employees all want to be associated with forward-thinking and innovative companies. Technology is not just a way to be more productive and efficient; it can completely transform your company's competitive position in the market.

Effective and innovative implementation of technology can be a significant driver of business value. All else equal, a company that leads its market in effective technology use will command a higher valuation. Period.

40.

Are Employee and Customer Safety a Priority at My Company?

Safety is a foundational issue in any merger or acquisition transaction today. Any company that uses equipment, fabricates raw materials, assembles components, lifts materials, or drives any type of vehicle, whether forklifts or luxury SUVs, on company business should be focused on safety. To do otherwise is to ignore risks that could impair even the strongest of balance sheets.

In 2016 a much larger publicly traded company approached one of our clients about acquiring their company. Before any financial information was shared or valuations discussed, the buyer concluded through initial and specific due diligence that our client had a strong and effective safety-first culture. Without this level of commitment to safety, the buyer would have moved on to another opportunity.

Granted, the transaction was in the engineering and construction industry, where safety has always been paramount. However, we are seeing an emphasis on employee and customer safety across nearly all industries, and many suppliers are now requiring proof of their vendors' commitment to safety before they will do business.

In a transaction to sell your business, you will likely need to demonstrate your commitment to safety via policy statements, injury reports to the Occupational Safety and Health Administration, training records, and workers' compensation filings.

You need to be ready from the beginning of the sales process to address this issue. If you wait, you will have to scramble to pull this data together or try to record it for the first time. For some buyers this is a threshold issue: your inability to provide sufficient information about your commitment to safety could have a detrimental effect on the prospective buyer's desire to move forward.

Most of all, of course, you should be committed to safety because it shows you value your employees and believe their well-being comes before company profits.

41.

Is My Company's Project Management Strong and Effective?

In our experience working with middle market and lower middle market companies, one of the most glaring weaknesses in these companies is the lack of a strong project management function.

These companies usually view project management as a cost and therefore both underinvest and underappreciate its potential value to their business. As a result, they experience surprise budget overruns and rarely learn from previous mistakes.

Another key cause of weak project management is that the company has failed to create a culture of accountability. Perhaps there is a lack of clarity around job responsibilities, as discussed in Question 32, growing pains associated with failing to adjust processes as the business grows, or a general disdain for meetings and putting people on the spot to answer for the status of their work.

That disdain for meetings and public accountability is often the product of management's prior experiences working for larger companies with more formal but still ineffective and time-consuming project management processes. We often see younger owners establish their businesses with a goal of creating the "anti-culture" from their prior experiences, not understanding that many processes used in larger organizations are necessary but were ineffectively executed.

An effective project management function will lead to more consistent profitability, more consistent product and service delivery, prevention of correctable errors, and a more stable work culture with fewer emergencies requiring staff to drop everything to fix a troubled project.

In a transaction scenario, the benefits of consistent profitability (meaning that the gross profit margins across most projects fall into an acceptable and understandable range) and the lack of a few dud jobs (projects with extremely low gross profit margins or even losses) is extremely valuable. Your EBITDA will be more consistent, and you will not be explaining why some projects are so profitable and some are not.

Another important benefit to good project management in a transaction scenario is the impact on the workforce. In organizations with a well-defined and well-executed project management function, the staff is less hurried, makes fewer mistakes, is more willing and able to follow important processes that provide for good internal controls and generate important operating data, and will be able to more effectively follow important safety protocols to minimize if not eliminate injuries. All these benefits bring value to your organization and will enhance and preserve value during the transaction process.

Contract, Tax, Regulatory, and Processes and Controls Questions to Ask Before You Sell Your Business

42.

Do I Properly Manage Risk in My Business?

Your contracts with vendors, customers, and other key parties will be highly scrutinized during the due diligence phase of a transaction.

The primary focus of this scrutiny will be to identify and understand the potential contractual obligations your business has assumed.

Such obligations include:

- Assumption of consequential damages for breach of contract

- Assumption of penalties for delayed delivery of goods or delayed systems startup, etc.

- Agreement to litigate contracts in unfavorable, distant, or even foreign jurisdictions

- Assumption of unfavorable terms and conditions from a master service agreement (such as one with a much larger company or government customer or in which you are not a party to the agreement)

- Bonding, license, and permit requirements

- Commitments to purchase certain quantities of goods or services

- Loss of material back-end rebates, marketing incentives, or discounted pricing should purchase levels not be met

- Drug testing and employee screening requirements that are well beyond industry standards

- Unfavorable payment terms

- Onerous insurance requirements

- Unreasonable warranty terms

- Non-industry-standard service level agreements or response times

- Time-consuming and expensive project status reporting requirements

- Lack of reasonable force majeure exclusions

This list could go on for several pages. The point is that prospective buyers will want to know and understand the risks they are assuming when they purchase your business.

When a buyer acquires your company, the purchase typically includes all your contracts with customers, vendors, service providers, landlords, and so on. Because the buyer will be effectively stepping into your place in these contracts, they will want to fully understand the benefits but even more importantly the performance obligations and potential liabilities included in the contracts. These potential liabilities include all the provisions of your contracts where you agree to be responsible for damages caused by your action or inaction or possibly even for the actions of other parties not in your control. Therefore, buyers will perform deep due diligence on all your contracts to ensure they understand the liabilities and obligations they are assuming.

To be clear, many of the risks associated with acquired contracts can be mitigated with deal terms or insurance. Buyers who are already a part of your industry may be able to renegotiate the contract or fold your business under an existing contract instead of assuming your contract's terms and conditions. But in some cases the buyer will have to decide whether to assume these contracts and their associated risks or move on to other potential transactions.

When contracting with customers, we recommend establishing a standard form contract. We recognize that many lower middle market and middle market companies contract regularly or even exclusively with Fortune 1000–size customers. In negotiating contracts with these customers, your company is clearly David up against Goliath's unlimited resources and strong market position. Even if this situation is normal business for you, we recommend creating a complete and fair standard contract to provide to all customers when negotiating a sale. Standard contracts benefit you because they:

- Ensure that special or unique terms used in your business are incorporated appropriately.

- Establish the negotiation of the contract on your terms and conditions. Even if you are contracting with a much larger organization, the ability to start the negotiations with your contract will improve your position or establish the importance of incorporating your business's specialized or unique terms and conditions.

- Improve efficiency, as contracts can be negotiated and closed with minimal or no legal costs.

- Close sales transactions more quickly, as some if not most customers will sign your contract form with little or no negotiation of terms and conditions.

- Create the standard processes and controls that are important to your business and improve quality because terms, conditions, and risks are consistent across your customer base.

- Imply your company is much larger and more sophisticated than it may really be.

- Establish payment and other key terms as if they are not negotiable.

- Significantly reduce due diligence time and expense when negotiating with lenders, insurance carriers, and certainly potential acquirers of your business.

For all other agreements with vendors and key partners, as well as nonstandard agreements with customers, we recommend designating a couple of key senior leaders who have been trained by your legal counsel and insurance carrier on the key legal terms in a contract so they can effectively identify problem issues. Many professional liability insurance carriers will provide some level of premium discount if company officials attend training on contractual risk and mitigation. Also, most business insurance brokers can advise you on the insurability of limitation of liability clauses, indemnities, and other tricky sections of business contracts.

Managing contractual risk is an important function in your day-to-day business, and it will also create value in the process of selling your business by reducing the buyer's risk and making the transaction easier to close.

43.

Are All of My Key Contracts In Force and Current?

In more and more industries, particularly in the services sector, contracts such as authorized service provider agreements, master service agreements, and fulfillment agreements are key value-drivers for the target company. Often, as companies get comfortable working together, the process of formally renewing agreements and keeping current key terms and conditions, such as pricing and service levels, goes by the wayside.

Pricing and some other details may be changed through email, conversation, or course of performance. While all of these may be legally enforceable, they may not be acceptable to a prospective buyer if the contract is a valuable asset of your company.

Buyers will want to ensure that all material contracts are in force and current when the transaction closes. If the contract has lapsed and the buyer forces you to negotiate a renewal, you will be at a decided disadvantage in those negotiations because the vendor or manufacturer will know you are desperate to get the contract updated and renewed.

Admittedly, forcing a renewal conversation has risks. It is not purely administrative in nature and could create challenging negotiations with customers or vendors seeking pricing improvements and other concessions that would never have been brought up had you just allowed the contract to continue, even if it had technically expired.

Conversely, there is risk in operating with an expired contract. For example, new leadership at the vendor or customer may take the opportunity of a contract's expired status to force a renegotiation or, worse, cancel it altogether without giving you the chance to discuss.

Furthermore, executing a strong contract administration function is a key ingredient to your overall risk-management system. Contracts should be reviewed and updated regularly for recent changes in laws and regulations regarding data security, data breaches, privacy, confidentiality of information, and employment. Regular attention to these matters sends a clear signal to customers, vendors, and even prospective buyers that you are actively managing the business and taking steps to mitigate potential risks.

Balancing the risks of having out-of-date contracts against forcing periodic renewals or amendments is a business decision only you can make based on the importance of the contract, your relationship with the other party, and the industry you operate in. If you are contemplating selling your business in the next few years, it will also pay to factor in the risks associated with entering the transaction process with expired key contracts.

44.

Do I Have Good Internal Controls Over My Company's Foreign Sales Activities?

The Foreign Corrupt Practices Act of 1977 (FCPA) makes it illegal to influence foreign officials with any personal payments or rewards.

If your company does business internationally, either directly or through sales agency agreements, you should have a stated policy that your business will comply with the FCPA. Additionally, your sales agent agreements should explicitly state that the agent is forbidden to engage in practices that violate the FCPA. Your policy and contractual agreements should be backed up by frequent training and reminders to both employees and sales agents that FCPA violations will not be tolerated.

For buyers experienced in international business and particularly publicly held or other larger buyers with significant reputational risk, the lack of clear compliance with FCPA could be a deal killer.

In Question 40, we mentioned a transaction in which the buyer, a much larger publicly held company, required an extensive initial understanding of our client's safety policy and record before they would enter into a letter of intent to purchase the company. The same was true for compliance with FCPA. This buyer reviewed our client's policy manual regarding FCPA compliance as well as all its agreements with foreign sales agents. Before this transaction closed, the buyer's legal counsel and an executive with our client traveled to Europe, Southeast Asia, and the Middle East to visit each sales agent face-to-face to gain final assurance that our client was serious about FCPA and that their international representatives were in compliance with the act.

Hopefully, you are intolerant of bad behavior in any part of your business, including bad actors who represent you and your company in foreign markets. Unfortunately, however, too many business owners have looked the other way when it comes to international business activities. They have an inkling or maybe even actual knowledge that improper payments or other rewards are being given, but they chalk it up to "That's what it takes to do business in that country" or "As long as it is just my agent doing it, then I won't be in trouble."

While these practices may not have had any negative impacts on your business to date, know that they could come back to haunt you when you are in the middle of the biggest sale of your life, the sale of your business.

45.

Does My Sales Order Management Process Ensure Effective Fulfillment?

In the course of day-to-day selling of your products and services, what happens immediately after the prospect says "yes" and issues a purchase order to buy something from your company?

Our experience reflects that after project management (Question 41), sales order management is the next most likely source of profit erosion related to operational execution.

Businesses that do not have a clear understanding of the scope of services to be performed; the products to be purchased, fabricated, assembled, delivered, and installed; the entity to be billed; and the time-frame for completion of the work will suffer a whole host of problems, such as poor customer satisfaction, profit erosion, and collections issues.

A strong sales order management process is a key value driver in a transaction to sell your company because it will show up either positively or negatively in your profitability and in your working capital. Buyers also know that these poor habits are particularly hard to break. Therefore, integrating your poor processes into theirs will be difficult. Or, in the case of a financial buyer wanting to bolt additional businesses on to yours, they know they will have to fix this process before they add even more sales volume to it.

Unfortunately, many companies underinvest in qualified personnel and adequate processes to effectively manage their sales orders. Instead, they rely on memory, familiarity, and hero effort to complete projects and eventually collect payments. They live with the consequences as a normal albeit dysfunctional aspect of their business.

Effective sales order management first requires creating a definition of a complete order, then not expending valuable resources to execute the order until that definition is met. Most companies consider the receipt of a customer purchase order as the definition of a sales order. This is only true if the following information is a part of the customer's order:

- The product(s) being purchased, including (as appropriate):

  - Model or size

  - Software revision level

  - Color

  - Optional features

  - Customer features

  - Complete description of the warranty, including the length of the warranty and when it commences

- Whether or not product updates are included

- Where installation will be performed

- The party responsible for the preparation of the installation location and what the requirements are to prepare the location

- The service(s) being purchased, including (as appropriate):
  - Complete description of the service(s) and any exclusions
  - Training, including how many individuals will be trained, where they will be trained, and how many times training will be offered
  - The deliverable associated with the services
  - The deadline(s) for the completion of the services
- The entity and address to be billed
- How the shipment and delivery of the products will occur and who is responsible for the associated costs of shipment
- Clarity of when title to the product(s) transfers to the customer and who is responsible for any damages to the product(s) during transit and installation of the product(s)

There are many more items that could be part of a clear definition of a sales order, depending upon the industry you operate in.

Unfortunately however, paranoia reigns in business, particularly around the sales process and securing orders from customers. Too often, companies are afraid to ask the customer the questions required to fully understand their needs and expectations for the project.

Consequently, companies must make assumptions to fill in the gaps, thereby short-cutting the process of assembling a complete order. Then they begin to mobilize resources and from that moment on struggle to catch up to the customer's expectations and timeline.

As the order is executed, telltale signs of order management problems emerge. The wrong color of the widget was ordered, or the wrong version of the software was installed. The company must make multiple trips to the location to correct errors. The customer has a much different expectation regarding training than the company budgeted for. Key items are missed entirely, causing whole sections of the work to be delayed and to be completed for no additional charge unless the customer can be convinced it was their fault. Finally, in the rush get the customer to "yes" and get the order started, no one confirmed the billing address, which is different than the installation address, so invoices went to the wrong location and sat for sixty days until the problem was discovered.

All these issues affect profitability, customer and employee satisfaction, and working capital. Therefore, these issues have an impact on the value of your company.

All of them could be avoided with stronger order management processes and an investment in the right people to execute them.

While not addressing these issues is unlikely to kill a transaction, weak sales order management processes could put those post-closing proceeds at risk if they are dependent on successful and rapid integration, profitability, or other operational factors.

46.

Do I Have Strong Physical and Digital Controls Around My IT Assets?

Your IT assets are a valuable, strategic element of your business, particularly if you have digitized your business model as we discussed in Question 39.

IT assets include your data networking systems, servers, storage systems, business applications, web addresses, websites, social media presence, and finally and most importantly, the data stored and used by those systems. As we have learned, businesses can be crippled and brand value severely diminished by failure to protect these assets.

Most prospective buyers will engage specialists to review your IT infrastructure, controls, and processes. This review will help them understand the risks in your current environment and the costs, if any, to upgrade your hardware and other systems to their standards.

Generally, these reviews are focused on identifying the challenges and potential benefits that may occur in integrating your IT assets into the buyer's systems or assessing the readiness of your systems for quick scalability.

However, in the case of an equity transaction in which the buyer will assume all your liabilities and risks, including those associated with how your IT assets have been operated and how well they have been controlled, there may be additional investigation and testing to determine that your data has not already been compromised unbeknownst to you. This additional scrutiny will be even more likely if you store consumers' personal information.

Here are five basic principles for business owners to help guide decision making about their IT assets:

- Assume your business is being attacked. Every business is under attack, no matter how small. Cyber-attacks are such a lucrative business and so easily and cost-effectively carried out by the bad guys that every business is being tested in multiple ways.

- Consider cloud services. For most small to middle market businesses, cloud services and third-party-hosted environments are more secure and more reliable than on-site equipment and employee-directed controls and protocols.

- Know that employees are the weakest link in IT security. Most networks maintained and secured by third-party professional data networking services companies are relatively impenetrable. However, no set of controls or protocols can stop cyber breaches if an employee unknowingly compromises their network credentials. Our IT consulting practice includes performing simulated phishing attempts and other social engineering tests to attempt to get employees to provide their logon credentials. They succeed in identifying the test threats more than 99 percent of the time. The bad guys are testing your employees every day as well.

- Consider employee education essential. Continuous education regarding your employees' role in cybersecurity should be a required task for everyone, including you, the owner. Cyber-attackers' methods are constantly evolving, so cybersecurity training should not be considered a "one-and-done" exercise.

- Invest in expertise. You must invest in IT security and follow up to ensure that you are getting what you are paying for. It is unlikely the solo computer whiz who takes care of desktop support can also design, implement, and ensure the continuous effectiveness of your IT security. Even if you have invested in a qualified and experienced IT director or a chief technology officer, it is likely you will still need to engage outside resources to help you stay current on these critical issues.

Following these five principles will make your business better today and will drive value and confidence into a transaction to sell your business. The most valuable business is one that can be used as a platform that can be scaled quickly. Creating a culture where IT assets are protected and valued as strategic assets is a key factor in positioning your company as a platform acquisition target.

47.

Do I Stay Current on My Business's Software Licenses?

In conjunction with the buyer's due diligence into IT assets and security discussed in Question 46, a prospective buyer will scan your network to identify all the software your business uses and to determine whether your software licenses are current.

A severe deficit in licensing could delay closing of your transaction while you work out fees and penalties with software providers, reductions in purchase price to cover the cost of bringing licenses up to date, or escrow of purchase proceeds while the issues are resolved.

Obviously, dealing with these issues during the due diligence process with a closing date looming will give you little leverage with software licensors in negotiating enterprise-wide or bulk licenses.

We strongly encourage business owners to run these scans on their networks periodically and know where their software licensing stands.

There are usually several takeaways from this exercise:

- The overall volume of applications. In most companies, there are three to five times the number of applications running on the network, or more likely on employee desktops, than the owner would have estimated.

- The extent of personal applications being used. Many of these unexpected applications running on your network or company computers are for personal use, such as iTunes, Netflix, Spotify, Canva (photo editing), personal banking, and social media applications. These applications, particularly streaming video services, may be using valuable bandwidth on your network, impacting network speed and reliability. You may have even purchased additional bandwidth to solve speed problems caused by these personal applications.

- Unauthorized business applications being used. Employees may have downloaded various productivity or collaboration applications for work without your knowledge. A few examples include Trello, Slack, Skype, Dropbox, or Asana. These programs may store customer, project, or sensitive employee data on their own servers, and often the trial, personal, or limited-use versions provide no guarantee regarding the security of the information stored there.

- The personal and rogue applications your IT department supports. Ask your IT staff or third-party desktop support provider for a report on the top applications driving support tickets to verify whether personal and rogue application installations are driving up support costs.

- Out-of-date applications licenses. You may discover that you have a licensing issue and need to take corrective action to bring licenses of key applications up to date. You may also find that you have stranded licenses that are not being used due to reductions in force or shifting of work to other applications. Ensure those licenses are not renewed or that no new licenses are obtained until the existing licenses are absorbed by new users.

The balance between business and personal use on company computers is highly dependent on the culture of your company, the industry you operate in, and outside factors such as data security protocols required in your business. In today's work anywhere, anytime, global business environment, it is unrealistic for most companies to lock down computers so that no additional applications can be downloaded. However, your company should create good governance and policies around the use of personal or other unauthorized business programs, particularly in relation to business data stored and transmitted through them.

48.

Do I Have Good Controls Over Company Purchasing Cards?

Included in the controls over purchasing and disbursements (see Question 28) should be good controls over company purchasing cards. Amazingly, in our practice, we often see clients who have a strong set of controls over their purchase-order process but give purchasing cards to a wide range of employees and neglect to review and approve their purchases. We literally see thousands of dollars in purchases being made with company cards, and no one in authority is bothering to look at the card statements to see what is being charged and by whom.

We were once engaged to provide transaction services to a company who had received a letter of intent to be purchased. Our client knew they had an inexperienced controller, and since they were being purchased by an international firm in their industry who would be engaging a "Big 4" international accounting firm to conduct due diligence, they wanted more accounting horsepower to help them through the transaction process. What they did not know was that their controller was both inexperienced in his role and addicted to gambling.

The latter issue might not have become a problem for the company, but, as the controller determined, management was not reviewing his purchasing card transactions. The controller figured out he could use his company card to withdraw cash from ATMs at his favorite gambling spots and not even have to worry about inventing an excuse—nobody in management would notice anyway. After only being on-site with the controller for about four hours, we had asked enough questions that he knew his ruse was over and he abruptly left the office and texted in his resignation over the lunch hour.

It did not take any great forensic talents to figure out this fraud. The company had simply failed to perform the most rudimentary oversight over the purchasing card transactions, and it cost them several hundred thousand dollars. Fortunately, we were able to help the client hold the proposed transaction together by demonstrating that the losses were isolated to one (former) employee and one transaction type.

Purchasing cards allow companies to streamline and reduce costs of processing smaller transactions. However, they can also enable employees to bypass internal controls over purchasing and disbursements when businesses fail to implement controls to ensure purchases made via credit card are authorized.

In addition to the potential loss of funds through fraud, owners risk loss of credibility with prospective buyers if the fraud is found during the due diligence phase of a transaction.

49.

Do I Maintain Good Maintenance Records on Key Manufacturing Equipment?

Any buyer's due diligence process will include verifying the maintenance and repair records for manufacturing equipment that is integral to your business.

The buyer will likely hire manufacturer-certified technicians to inspect equipment and the associated maintenance records. In a manufacturing environment, these inspections are a critical piece of due diligence. Buyers want to avoid surprises, especially ones with big price tags such as deferred maintenance or finding out after the fact that a warranty has been voided due to improper maintenance or usage.

Some companies fail to keep accurate and complete records on the maintenance of their manufacturing assets, a practice that could come back to haunt them.

Like similar issues, this matter is unlikely to derail a transaction. However, it will be tedious and time-consuming to catch up these records during due diligence. More importantly, it will likely subtract from the buyer's confidence in the quality of the seller's record-keeping and raise questions about what other corners are being cut that might create problems in the future.

50.

Is My Company in Compliance With All Applicable Tax Reporting Requirements?

The transaction to sell your business will be memorialized by a contract, often titled the Definitive Purchase Agreement, the Asset Purchase Agreement, the Stock Purchase Agreement, the Membership Interest Purchase Agreement, or any of a few other names, depending upon the corporate structure of your business and the structure of the transaction. Regardless of the name of the agreement, it will contain a key section labeled "Seller's Representations and Warranties." As the transaction proceeds toward finalization and this contract takes shape, we encourage sellers to schedule a meeting with all of their key professionals to review these representations in detail to be sure each affirmative representation can be made with confidence and that any exceptions are appropriately identified and disclosed.

One of the key representations you will be asked to make is regarding the filing of all applicable tax returns in all jurisdictions, like this sample representation at find-law.com/smallbusiness:

> *"The Company has filed all tax returns required to have been filed. All such tax returns were correct and complete in all material respects. All taxes owed by the*

Company (whether or not shown on any tax return) have been paid or provid-
ed for in the Company's financial statements. The Company currently is not the
beneficiary of any extension of time within which to file any tax return. To the
Company's knowledge, no claim has ever been made by an authority in a jurisdic-
tion where the Company does not file tax returns that it is or may be subject
to taxation by that jurisdiction. There are no actual, pending or, to the Company's
knowledge, threatened liens, encumbrances, or charges against any of the assets
of the Company arising in connection with any failure (or alleged failure) to pay
any tax."

Most businesses stay on top of their federal tax filing obligations as well as those of their home state. However, many businesses fail to grasp the complexities and reach of other state and local jurisdictions' tax statutes.

State and local tax law (known as "SALT" in accounting circles) is a highly complex area of taxation and usually requires the assistance of experts to determine whether your business's operating activities create tax liabilities in various jurisdictions.

Many companies wrongly assume that because they do not have a physical presence in the form of an office and local employees, they are therefore not technically doing business in that state. In fact, most states' SALT statutes have a much broader definition than physical presence. Furthermore, the Supreme Court's North Dakota v. Wayfair, Inc. decision in June 2018 created an entirely new concept called "economic nexus" such that the volume of business, not just physical presence or in-state employees, can be used as a basis for imposing the collection of sales tax on an out-of-state company. Over time, most states are expected to adopt legislation similar to North Dakota's, and many more companies, not just online companies, will therefore be required to charge, collect, and remit sales taxes on their out-of-state sales.

If your company does business with companies in other states, we strongly recommend you seek advice from a SALT expert to determine if you may be required to comply with tax statutes in those states.

SALT issues are a significant point of emphasis in acquisition transactions, particularly among experienced participants, because the issue surfaces in so many transactions. The potential liabilities from failure to file returns and pay taxes along with penalties and interest can easily reach hundreds of thousands if not millions of dollars.

When these issues arise in due diligence, they can delay a deal and often result in the creation of escrows or holdbacks so that buyers can allow these issues to be resolved through catching up compliance or through the expiration of statutes of limitations. If the tax compliance issues are overwhelming, some buyers will put the transaction on hold until they can be resolved, which of course introduces risk that the transaction will never close.

51.

Do I Have Hidden or Ignored Environmental Liabilities?

If real estate will be included in the sale of your company or if your business works with hazardous materials, you should take steps to ensure you are compliant with all applicable environmental laws before embarking on a transaction.

Environmental issues will cause deals to stall and often kill them altogether.

Almost all transactions involving real estate, including transactions to sell a business with real estate, involve financing from a lender. Lenders are required by law to have Phase I Environmental Site Assessment completed prior to closing on a loan to finance the property.

According to Partner Engineering and Science, Inc., the purpose of a Phase I is to "research the current and historical uses of a property as part of a commercial real estate transaction. The intent of the report is to assess if the current or historical property uses have impacted the soil or groundwater beneath the property and could pose a threat to the environment and/or human health. If issues are found, it presents a potential liability to the owner and impacts the value of the property." A recent Phase I is required in any real estate transaction involving a lender.

According to Partner Engineering and Science, Inc., a Phase I typically includes:

- "A site visit to observe current and past conditions and uses of the property and adjacent properties;

- A review of governmental regulatory databases including, but not limited to, underground storage tanks, above ground storage tanks, known or suspected release cases, the storage of hazardous substances, and disposal of hazardous wastes including petroleum products, and institutional and engineering controls;

- A review of historical records, such as historical aerial photographs, fire insurance maps (Sanborn maps), historical city directories, and historical topographic maps;

- A review of state and local agency records, including but not limited to state environmental agencies, Building Departments, Fire Departments, and Health Departments;

- Interviews with current and past property owners, operators, occupants, or others familiar with the property;

- Interviews with the Report User for title or judicial records for environmental liens and activity and use limitations; specialized knowledge or experience, actual knowledge, commonly known or reasonably ascertainable information, the reason for a significantly lower purchase price; and the reason for the preparation of the Phase I ESA."

The environmental professional or firm engaged to conduct the Phase I will present its findings to the client, usually a lender or the property owner. If there are no findings requiring further investigation, property ownership can be transferred and the lenders will usually be comfortable providing financing for the real estate purchase, which may be a part of the overall transaction to purchase your business.

If issues are found in the Phase I, the process proceeds to a Phase II Environmental Site Assessment. The Phase II assessment determines the presence or absence of petroleum products or hazardous waste in the site subsurface by testing soil borings. If harmful materials are found, further tests are usually conducted, and a remediation plan is prepared and executed.

Professionals who have worked in the mergers and acquisition space for any length of time have been surprised by an environmental issue just as a deal was moving toward closing. Consequently, many investment bankers and business brokers serving the middle market require the seller to have a Phase I study completed before starting the sales process to prevent deals from being stalled or killed from an environmental issue discovered later.

Do not ignore an environmental issue if you know you have one. To do so is unethical and most likely illegal. Furthermore, the professional standards, quality controls, and processes put in place by the professionals and lenders who support merger and acquisition transactions will insist that these issues be confronted before allowing a transaction to close.

52.

If I Operate Multiple Legal Entities for Tax and Liability Purposes, Do I Maintain Well-Documented Legal Separation Between Them?

Most lower middle market and middle market businesses operate as limited liability companies or as corporations. Using one of these structures limits the exposure of the owners' personal assets from liabilities incurred by the business. By setting up multiple legal entities, owners can shield each company's assets from the liabilities and damages that might arise in another company.

For example, we have a client that has two primary businesses. One business designs and installs data and voice networking infrastructure in commercial buildings; the other modifies the equipment on cell towers to enable new technologies such as high-speed transmission of voice and data. This client established two separate legal entities for these two businesses because their risk profiles are separate and distinct. By doing so, the assets of the networking company as well as the owner's personal assets are protected from liabilities and damages that might occur in the much higher-risk cell tower modification company.

There are many other potential benefits of a multi-entity structure for your businesses. Of course, there are also downsides to many of these strategies as well. Those discussions are outside the scope of this book.

However, one of the clear benefits of these multi-entity legal structures in a transaction scenario is the ease of selling one business while retaining other businesses. Segregating accounting and tax records by legal entity and business line enables the owner to more easily present the true financial results of the business to prospective buyers.

However, to achieve this benefit, as well as any other potential benefits, owners must truly keep the business affairs of each company separate through proper contracting, accounting, business operations, and observance of corporate formalities such as annual officer election, board minutes supporting key decisions or transactions, and annual owner meetings. Too often, owners spend significant resources setting up these structures and then operate as if they were all one company, risking the very benefits they were seeking to achieve.

Contracting is one of the most important elements of this principle. You will need to ensure that when Company A contracts to sell something to a customer, Company A's name is on the contract and Company A's authorized officer signs it.

Another key aspect of maintaining the efficacy of these structures is respecting the capitalization of each company as cash is moved between companies and distributed to ownership. If it appears that cash (capital) is transferred between the entities or to the owners such that one or more entities are purposely kept insolvent to prevent creditors or other claimants from being able to recover losses, then those creditors may be able to disregard the legal entity and access cash held by other entities or by the owners themselves.

We do not practice law, but in our experience, it is very difficult for creditors or other claimants to "pierce the corporate veil" and successfully reach the assets of a parent or sister company. That said, we advise clients to carefully observe corporate formalities to ensure the desired protections and other benefits are preserved and that claimants are not tempted to pursue this strategy.

The word "tempted" is important. If you are sloppy with your corporate governance and in operating your companies, claimants who believe they have been significantly damaged may take the risk and elect to litigate to access your personal assets or the assets of other companies. While you will likely win this issue in the end, it will not feel like it after you have spent tens of thousands or possibly hundreds of thousands of dollars and enormous amounts of your time and energy to do so. It is best to do things right from the beginning.

In a transaction, it is imperative that the legal and accounting records reflect the true operations and financial results of each company. If ordinary business transactions or owner transactions are mingled together across companies as if they were all the same business, it will be expensive and time-consuming to straighten it all out. You will run the risk of the prospective buyer moving on to another opportunity or losing trust that they will ever receive accurate financial records for the business they are trying to buy.

53.

Do I Have a List of All Leases My Company Is Party to?

Leases on office, warehouse, and manufacturing space and on equipment often represent the most significant future obligation of a business. Lease obligations can represent future cash outlays of hundreds of thousands or even millions of dollars.

Consequently, prospective buyers will want to fully understand the obligations they will assume if they purchase your business. The buyer's strategic direction of the company may vary greatly from yours, and that direction may include the need for much more warehouse, manufacturing, or office space than your current facilities. The buyer may also want to consolidate operations of your company with their existing operations, or they may intend to move your operations to a new location, rendering your current leased space useless to them.

The number of leases, the remaining terms on those leases, their pricing, and how they fit with the buyer's growth strategies can be enormous considerations in negotiation of a transaction.

We recommend maintaining a database of all your leases, including start and end dates, monthly payment amounts, escalator and renewal clauses, and other key terms. You will have to assemble this list in due diligence, and it will be to your advantage to understand the details of your leasing portfolio before you begin the transaction process.

Under recently enacted accounting rules, nearly all leases with a term greater than one year will have to be recorded as liabilities on the balance sheet. For most companies, the most significant impact of this accounting change will be to record their leases for office, manufacturing, warehousing, and all other space as "right-to-use" assets with a corresponding liability. When this new rule is fully implemented by both publicly held and private companies, the assets and liabilities on almost all company balance sheets will increase significantly to reflect leasing transactions.

Given you will likely need to assemble a database of your current leases to satisfy these new accounting rules, you will have already gathered the information needed regarding leases when you begin the process of selling your business.

54.

Are My Employee Benefit Cost-Sharing Ratios Current With the Market?

Once the financial details of a business sale begin to come together, the parties will quickly begin to analyze some initial integration issues. An important part of this analysis will be to compare the employee benefits offered by each company and determine the pros and cons for your company's employees as they are absorbed into the buyer's benefit plans.

In general, buyers are usually larger organizations and will have comparable or more robust benefit offerings. These enhanced offerings might include more medical plan options, more voluntary benefits, and nonstandard offerings such as long-term care insurance or prepaid legal services.

However, while the buyer often has an enhanced suite of benefits available, the seller may have shouldered a greater proportion of the cost of the benefits they have offered. Smaller companies are notorious for paying a larger share of medical insurance premiums as well as continuing to offer plans with lower-than-market deductibles and lower-than-market out-of-pocket limits.

In this scenario, without any adjustment to compensation, the seller's employees could experience a reduction in take-home pay on day one of the acquisition. It will be very difficult to energize and excite the seller's employee base about the future unless the buyer addresses this issue in a meaningful way.

Most likely, offering a good employee benefit package and paying a higher-than-market portion of the costs of those benefits is a strategy to be able to attract and retain key talent to your organization.

We advise clients in this position to carefully consider their benefit packages, including key aspects such as cost-sharing ratios, deductible levels, and out-of-pocket maximums, to ensure they do not fall too far behind the market. As every owner knows, benefits costs are a major expense and can be volatile year to year as markets and regulations change. There should be ample opportunity to keep pace with the market for key benefit provisions while still offering plans that will attract and retain talent to your organization.

We would not expect any owner to give up this strategy of attracting talent in contemplation of a sale of the business that may not occur for several years. However, owners should see value in keeping pace with the market so that an eventual integration of your workforce with another organization sees as little disruption as possible.

Do not forget that in many transactions in the middle market and lower middle market space, large portions of the purchase price are paid or earned after the closing, so it will be in your best interest to help ensure a smooth integration of your workforce into the buyer's organization.

55.

Is My Business Nimble and Resilient Enough to Withstand Potential Disruption?

Middle market businesses often hit a home run with a single product or service, with a single customer, or in a single industry. When times are good, the owner has his hands full keeping up with orders and dealing with the inherent issues of running a business. But things inevitably change. Industries go through down cycles, new technologies come into the market, and customers' needs change. When these changes happen, smaller businesses are often casualties.

If your business is one of those smaller ones most at risk in a time of industry change, building resiliency into your business model, though challenging, is worth consideration, experimentation, and thoughtful investment.

Businesses that have a demonstrated ability to generate revenues in down economic cycles or have successfully pivoted into different industries are more valuable than those that just ride the ups and downs of a single industry. Achieving this kind of diversification is not easy and not always possible, but owners should take some time at least annually to get away from the business and think about additional applications of their products and services, other potential products that could be manufactured using the same equipment, or other markets that could be served.

During this annual review, owners should consider working through a SWOT analysis with either their leadership team or with an outside, unbiased advisor. A SWOT analysis will force you to list and carefully consider your company's strengths, weaknesses, opportunities, and threats. If approached with honesty and transparency, a SWOT analysis will likely elicit one or more "aha" moments. You might discover a new opportunity you had not considered before or come face-to-face with a threat that has crept up on you while your head has been down running the business.

You may also want to set aside 2 to 5 percent of your profits to invest in experimentation and innovation. Most great innovations come from the field, from the users of products, services, and systems. In addition, innovations are often born out of limited resources. A scarcity of resources usually drives more effective solutions than does a big, costly team with a large budget. Tasking small groups of users with limited resources, even as little as $500, can generate transformative results.

The goal is to routinely take time to think objectively about your business and invest in improving it, to see your business from your customers', vendors', and employees' points of view and initiate the changes that will make your business better, more resilient, and ready for the future—including its future sale.

Closing
Thoughts

No business is perfect.

In fact, most businesses, even highly successful and profitable ones, are dysfunctional in some way, if not in many ways. You will be addressing and readdressing these 55 Questions—and other issues—continuously throughout your leadership of your organization.

Thankfully, dysfunctional businesses are successfully purchased and sold every day. You do not have to wait until you have addressed each of our questions or fixed every problem to sell your business. That day would never come.

Yes, buyers prefer and place value on well-run, highly functional businesses, but they too know that no business is perfect. In truth, strategic buyers, those companies in your industry that are much larger and seemingly much more sophisticated, are also grappling with the issues addressed in these 55 Questions. You may be successfully purchased by a much larger company only to find out during integration of your company into theirs that they have bigger problems than you do.

So do not despair. Work hard on your business. Use these questions to challenge yourself, your company's culture, and your employees to get better every day.

There will be a payoff for your hard work. Your company will be better today while you own it, as well as later, when it is time to sell. Take comfort that while your work will never be fully complete, you made your business as valuable as you possibly could. There will be a buyer out there who will pay you for what you have built and then start their own journey to make it bigger and better.

Appendix

Appendix A

Normalization of Target Company Cash Flows

Goal of Normalization: The goal of normalizing the target company's cash flows is to estimate the future cash flows of the business under new ownership. The calculation starts by adjusting after-tax net income of the business to Earnings Before Interest, Taxes, Depreciation, and Amortization (EBITDA) and then adjusting EBITDA for discretionary items and non-recurring items. The result approximates the true cash flows generated by the business in the periods presented.

The calculation removes the impact of how the business is capitalized, discretionary expenses which are not required to operate the business then adjusts current expenses which do not represent fair market value for the services received, and removes the impact of one-time, non-recurring revenues or expenses which are unlikely to be repeated in the future.

The table below provides examples of the calculation of adjusted EBITDA as well as some of the more common normalization adjustments.

		Sample Company, LLC Adjusted EBITDA Calculation December 31, 2019			
		12/31/2017		12/31/2018	12/31/2019
EBITDA:					
After-tax Net Income	$	550,000	$	1,753,510	$ 2,370,950
Plus: Interest		3,270		286,400	
Plus: Income Taxes		213,889		681,921	922,036
Plus: Depreciation		301,438		285,920	175,430
Plus: Amortization		462		650	250
EBITDA		1,069,059		3,008,401	3,468,666
Normalization Adjustments:					
Owner Discretionary Expense Adjustments:					
Plus: Rent Expense		1,880		18,840	27,500
Less: Fair Market Value Rent Expense				(16,140)	(23,430)
Plus: Charitable Contributions		2,000		3,890	7,500
Less: Officer Compensation				(175,000)	(180,000)
Less: Shared Office Staff Compensation				(38,000)	(40,000)
Less: Shared Utilities Expense				(3,700)	(4,600)
Plus: Private Plane Expense				146,000	175,000
Total Owner Discretionary Expense Adjustments		3,880		(64,110)	(38,030)
Nonrecurring Items:					
Less: Interest Income		(100)		(42,900)	(120)
Less: Gain on Sale of Equipment				(45,000)	
Plus: Business Development Expense		-		27,630	
Less: Legal Settlement					(50,000)
Total Nonrecurring Items		(100)		(60,270)	(50,120)
Adjusted EBITDA	$	1,072,839		2,884,021	3,380,516

EBITDA Adjustments

The calculation of EBITDA is usually straight-forward. Interest, income taxes, depreciation, and amortization expenses are added back to net income to arrive at EBITDA.

EBITDA is considered a proxy for the cash flows of the operations of the company without the impacts of how the company has been capitalized, i.e., with debt or equity financing or a combination of the two. It allows for easier comparison of company results against other companies both inside and outside of the same industry.

Owner Discretionary Expense Adjustments

Owner discretionary expenses are cash outlays made by the current owner of the target business which are not required to operate the business in its normal course. Examples include non-market rent payments, charitable contributions, above or below fair market compensation to the owner or the owner's family members, country club memberships, sports stadium suite rentals, and the cost of owning and operating a private plane.

Rent Expense: The current owner of the business is often paying rent to himself which may or may not reflect current market rates. The new owner has the choice to either move to a new space or negotiate a fair market value of rent. The amount of rent expense reflected in the financial statements is added back to EBITDA so that the current market rate for rent can be deducted to properly normalize rent expense - see next item.

Fair Market Value Rent Expense: After adding back the rent expense reflected in the current owner's financial statements (see item above), the fair market value of rent for the business is deducted from EBITDA to normalize rent expense for the business.

Charitable Contributions: Charitable contributions are considered discretionary expenses of the owner and not required to operate the business. Therefore, they are usually added back to EBITDA in the normalization process.

Officer Compensation: In this example, the target company was not paying the owner a salary even though he was leading the company on a day-to-day basis. To normalize officer compensation, a market salary appropriate for the size and complexity of the business is deducted in the EBITDA normalization calculation.

Shared Office Staff Compensation: In this example, the owner of the target company operated two businesses and engaged one employee to perform administrative tasks for both companies. This deduction reflects the approximate cost of an administrative professional for the targeted business.

Shared Utilities Expense: Similar to the shared office staff compensation item above, this deduction represents the approximate utilities cost of the target business operated separately from the owner's other business.

Private Plane Expense: Typically, the cost of owning and operating a private plane is a discretionary expense of the owner and is therefore added back to normalize EBITDA of the business.

Non-recurring Items

Non-recurring adjustments include transactions not in the normal course of operations that are included in the historical operating results of the target company. The value of these transactions is added to or subtracted from the target's financial statements to produce EBITDA representative of the day-to-day, normal operations of the company.

Interest Income Discussion: Interest income is deducted from EBITDA because it reflects the company's choice to maintain cash balances, usually excess cash balances, as part of its capital structure rather than reinvesting the cash in the business or distributing the cash to the owner(s). Similar to interest expense, interest income is removed from EBITDA to enable comparison to other companies who capitalize the business with other forms of financing.

Gain on Sale of Equipment: One-time gains on the sale of equipment are deducted to normalize EBITDA because the sale of equipment is an unusual and infrequent transaction for the company. Including the gain in EBITDA would overstate the cash flows generated from normal operations.

Business Development Expense: Unusually large business development expenses are added back to EBITDA if they represent an infrequent event. For example, if in one of the historical years' financial statements the target company had purchased a hospitality tent at the U.S. Open golf championship to entertain customers, that infrequent expense would be added back to adjusted EBITDA.

Legal Settlement: Legal settlements, either payments or receipts, are typically added back or deducted, respectively, from EBITDA because they are non-recurring in nature and do not reflect the normal operations of the business. Note that if the target company routinely received monetary settlements by pursuing legal action to enforce its patents or other intellectual property rights, then such settlements should be included in normalized EBITDA as a regular outcome of the operations of the company.

References

QUESTION 8

In an article for *investmentbank.com:* Nead, Nate. "How to Maximize Your Sale Price in Mergers & Acquisitions." InvestmentBank.com, InvestmentBank, 20 Oct. 2020, investmentbank.com/maximize/.

QUESTION 14

the oft-quoted statistic that 88 percent of spreadsheets contain a mathematical error: Panko, Raymond R. "What We Know About Spreadsheet Errors." *Journal of Organizational and End User Computing,* vol. 10, no. 2, 1998, pp. 15–21., doi:10.4018/joeuc.1998040102.

QUESTION 18

In a piece for Forbes: Bradt, George. "How to Turn Seasonality into a Competitive Advantage." Forbes, *Forbes Magazine,* 1 July 2015, www.forbes.com/sites/george-bradt/2015/07/01/how-to-turn-seasonality-into-a-competitive-advantage/.

Newell Brands, the parent company of Elmer's Glue: Popken, Ben. "Parents Stuck Searching for Glue as Kids Go Crazy for 'Slime'." *NBCNews.com*, NBCUniversal News Group, 28 Feb. 2017, www.nbcnews.com/business/consumer/parents-stuck-searching-glue-kids-go-crazy-slime-n726256.

QUESTION 31

Mergers and acquisitions advisor Steven Pappas of Touchstone Advisors stated: Pappas, Steven. "The Strategic Buyer vs. Financial Buyer: How Do They Differ?" *TouchstoneAdvisors.com*, Touchstone Advisors, 13 Aug. 2020, touchstoneadvisors.com/strategic-buyer-vs-financial-buyer/.

QUESTION 33

We recommend a "feedforward" approach: Cooper, Robert K. "Feedforward." *Get Out of Your Own Way: The 5 Keys to Surpassing Everyone's Expectations*, Crown Publishing Group, 2006, pp. 175–176.

QUESTION 36

Robert Sher, founding principal of CEO to CEO…stated in a piece for Forbes: Sher, Robert. "Why Half of All M&A Deals Fail, and What You Can Do About It." *Forbes*, Forbes Magazine, 19 Mar. 2012, www.forbes.com/sites/forbesleadershipforum/2012/03/19/why-half-of-all-ma-deals-fail-and-what-you-can-do-about-it.

QUESTION 39

Tirrell Payton, a San-Diego-based technology consultant writing for business.com, states: Payton, Tirrell. "Why Every Company Is a Tech Company." *business.com*, business.com, 14 Jan. 2015, www.business.com/articles/why-every-company-is-a-technology-company/.

QUESTION 50

like this sample representation at findlaw.com: FindLaw Team, "Sample Representations And Warranties." *Findlaw.com*, FindLaw, 16 Feb. 2018, www.findlaw.com/smallbusiness/closing-a-business/sample-representations-and-warranties.html.

QUESTION 51

According to Partner Engineering and Science, Inc., the purpose of a Phase I is to: Redlin, Jenny. "What Is a Phase I Environmental Site Assessment." *Partneresi.com*, Partner Engineering and Science, Inc., 9 Apr. 2018, www.partneresi.com/resources/blog/what-is-a-phase-i-environmental-site-assessment.